HIKING THE PACIFIC CREST TRAIL – OREGON AND WASHINGTON

PCT – CASTELLA TO MANNING PARK

by David Jordan

JUNIPER HOUSE, MURLEY MOSS,
OXENHOLME ROAD, KENDAL, CUMBRIA LA9 7RL
www.cicerone.co.uk

First edition 2025
ISBN: 978 1 78631 214 3

Printed in China on responsibly sourced paper on behalf of Latitude Press Ltd.
A catalogue record for this book is available from the British Library.
All photographs are by the author unless otherwise stated.

Route mapping by Lovell Johns www.lovelljohns.com
Contains OpenStreetMap.org data © OpenStreetMap contributors, CC-BY-SA.
NASA relief data courtesy of ESRI

Updates to this guide

While every effort is made by our authors to ensure the accuracy of guidebooks as they go to print, changes can occur during the lifetime of an edition. Any updates that we know of for this guide will be on the Cicerone website (www.cicerone.co.uk/1212/updates), so please check before planning your trip. We also advise that you check information about such things as transport, accommodation and shops locally. Even rights of way can be altered over time. We are always grateful for information about any discrepancies between a guidebook and the facts on the ground, sent by email to updates@cicerone.co.uk.

Register your book: To sign up to receive free updates, special offers and GPX files where available, create a Cicerone account and register your purchase via the 'My Account' tab at www.cicerone.co.uk

Front cover: The ridgeline of Goat Rocks a spectacular traverse with Mount Rainier ahead (Stage 88)

CONTENTS

Mount Rainier beyond the Lily Basin (Stage 88)

Warning

The Pacific Crest Trail is designed as a summer trail to be hiked when it is free of snow and the creeks are relatively low. You should be aware that navigation could be difficult and the trail could be dangerous when there is snow in the mountains or when the creeks are running high because of snowmelt. The maps in this guide will not be adequate for navigation when snow covers the trail. If you hike the PCT you will be going into high mountains, wilderness areas and deserts. You might be faced with severe storms, fording unbridged creeks, wildfires, burned areas and hiking through long waterless sections in high temperatures. Mountains and wilderness trekking can be dangerous, carrying the risk of personal injury or death.

Note on mapping

The route maps in this guide are derived from publicly available data, databases and crowd-sourced data. As such they have not been through the detailed checking procedures that would generally be applied to a published map from an official mapping agency. However, we have reviewed them closely in the light of local knowledge as part of the preparation of this guide.

Mountain safety

Every mountain walk has its dangers, and those described in this guidebook are no exception. All who walk or climb in the mountains should recognise this and take responsibility for themselves and their companions along the way. The author and publisher have made every effort to ensure that the information contained in this guide was correct when it went to press, but, except for any liability that cannot be excluded by law, they cannot accept responsibility for any loss, injury or inconvenience sustained by any person using this book.

International distress signal *(emergency only)*
Six blasts on a whistle (and flashes with a torch after dark) spaced evenly for one minute, followed by a minute's pause. Repeat until an answer is received. The response is three signals per minute followed by a minute's pause.

Helicopter rescue
The following signals are used to communicate with a helicopter:

Help needed: raise both arms above head to form a 'Y'

Help not needed: raise one arm above head, extend other arm downward

Emergency telephone numbers
In the US the Nationwide Emergency Number is 911

Be prepared to confirm:
1. The location of the emergency
2. The phone number you are calling from
3. The type of the emergency
4. The detail of the emergency

The operator will then transfer you to the appropriate response team.

Weather reports
National Weather Service: www.weather.gov
Mountain Weather: www.mountain-forecast.com

Mountain rescue can be very expensive – be adequately insured.

The trail above Bull Lake in Castle Crags State Park (Stage 56)

ROUTE SUMMARY TABLE –

(FROM INTERSTATE 5 AT CASTELLA TO THE NORTHERN TERMINUS)

No.	Stage	Distance (miles)	Total ascent (feet)	Total descent (feet)	Duration (hr:min)	Page
Section 7						
56	I-5 (Castella) – Parks Creek Rd	38.5	7165	2451	19:00	17
57	Parks Creek Rd – Hwy 3	20.5	886	2372	8:00	19
58	Hwy 3 – Carter Meadows Summit	19.8	3077	2283	9:10	21
59	Carter Meadows Summit – Etna Summit	19.7	3789	4019	9:50	23
60	Etna Summit – Paradise Lake	29.1	5387	5223	13:55	25
61	Paradise Lake – Seiad Valley	27.1	1886	6706	10:00	26
62	Seiad Valley – Cook and Green Pass	14.8	5157	1762	9:35	28
63	Cook and Green Pass – Wrangle Gap	27.6	4954	3228	13:00	30
64	Wrangle Gap – I-5 (Ashland)	20.4	1831	4062	8:30	34
Totals		**217.5**	**34,132**	**32,106**	**101:00**	
Section 8						
65	I-5 Ashland – Hyatt Lake	23.9	3776	2835	10:00	42
66	Hyatt Lake – Dead Indian Memorial Rd	18.9	2812	2536	8:10	44
67	Dead Indian Memorial Rd – Red Lake Trail	25.2	2667	2047	10:15	47
68	Red Lake Trail – Sevenmile Trail	17.4	1877	2172	7:25	49
69	Sevenmile Trail – Hwy 62	16.8	1969	1604	7:40	51
70	Hwy 62 – Hwy 138	26.9	1850	2083	10:00	53
71	Hwy 138 – Windigo Pass	30.4	3330	3445	12:30	55
72	Windigo Pass – Williamette Pass	29.7	3294	4012	12:30	56
73	Williamette Pass – Irish Lake	22.7	2753	2277	9:30	60
74	Irish Lake – Horse Lake Trail (Elk Lake)	23.2	1486	1755	8:50	63
75	Horse Lake Trail (Elk Lake) – Hwy 242 McKenzie Pass	29.9	3894	3927	12:55	64
Totals		**265**	**29,708**	**28,693**	**109:45**	

No.	Stage	Distance (miles)	Total ascent (feet)	Total descent (feet)	Duration (hr:min)	Page
Section 9						
76	Hwy 242 McKenzie Pass – Santiam Pass	17.1	1739	2201	7:10	73
77	Santiam Pass – Milk Creek	27.6	3737	4134	12:25	75
78	Milk Creek – Breitenbush Lake	12.2	2697	1542	6:30	77
79	Breitenbush Lake – Road 42	34.4	2851	4885	14:05	79
80	Road 42 – Barlow Pass	18.1	2001	1293	7:25	83
81	Barlow Pass to Lolo Pass	22.7	4439	5207	11:15	85
82	Lolo Pass – Wahtum Lake	16.4	2244	1768	6:40	87
83	Wahtum Lake – I-84 Cascade Locks	16.1	2005	5620	7:00	86
Totals		**164.6**	**21,713**	**26,650**	**72:30**	
Section 10						
84	I-84 Cascade Locks – Wind River Rd	33.3	6447	5571	15:55	95
85	Wind River Rd – Road 24	34.8	6152	2999	16:00	97
86	Road 24 – Road 23	14.1	1808	2159	6:15	101
87	Road 23 – Road 5603	22.2	3038	2198	10:20	102
88	Road 5603 – Hwy12 near White Pass	43.8	6709	7116	21:15	105
89	Hwy 12 near White Pass – Chinook Pass	28.6	4580	3550	14:45	106
90	Chinook Pass – Road 784	32	4327	4833	13:50	111
91	Road 784 – Stampede Pass	19.4	3383	4626	8:30	112
92	Stampede Pass – I-90 Snoqualmie Pass	18.3	3268	3973	8:20	115
Totals		**246.5**	**39,712**	**37,025**	**115:10**	

No.	Stage	Distance (miles)	Total ascent (feet)	Total descent (feet)	Duration (hr:min)	Page
Section 11						
93	I-90 Snoqualmie Pass – Waptus River	34.7	7549	7467	18:55	122
94	Waptus River – Stevens Pass	36.2	7474	6476	19:40	125
95	Stevens Pass – Indian Pass	34.2	7041	6148	17:00	126
96	Indian Pass – Suiattle River	42.3	8107	10,696	19:50	131
97	Suiattle River – Stehekin River	31.3	5000	5850	13:20	132
98	Stehekin River – Rainy Pass	19.3	4580	1325	9:20	134
99	Rainy Pass – Hart's Pass	30.9	5922	4577	14:50	137
100	Hart's Pass – Northern Terminus	30.5	4485	6424	14:30	139
Totals		**259.4**	**50,158**	**48,963**	**127:25**	
	Exit from Northern Terminus – Manning Park	8.8	1112	1457	4:00	140

INTRODUCTION

Starting from the Mexican border, at a monument around 50 miles east of San Diego, the Pacific Crest Trail (PCT) meanders its way north for around 2655 miles, through the combined length of California, Oregon and Washington, all the way to a corresponding monument at the Canadian Border about 100 miles east of Vancouver, British Columbia. As the name suggests, it follows the crest of the mountains, rising and falling with the watershed divide, exploring the panorama that becomes visible, only from the higher ground.

This is book three in a series that also includes: book one – *Hiking the Pacific Crest Trail*, and book two – *Hiking the Pacific Crest Trail – California*. The guide has been presented as three booklets to enable the hiker to keep weight to the absolute minimum, while still carrying a physical guide and maps that can both supplement, and if necessary, replace a digital mapping app.

In planning terms, the PCT is too long to think about in its entirety, not least as it includes incredibly diverse landscapes and conditions, which affect choices of gear, time of year, when and where to resupply, right down to where to camp and find adequate water. It is necessary to break the trail down into manageable chunks, to facilitate hiking in sections, or as a way of planning the logistics of a thru-hike.

This guide divides the trail into 100 stages grouped into 11 sections. The structure hopes to offer the section hiker an easier way to plan and think about smaller hikes, that can easily be 'chunked' together when more time is available for longer outings. At the same time the thru-hiker might appreciate the manageable scale that encourages them to think, typically a day or two ahead in each stage while tent sites and water sources are the priority, yet still relate to a larger structure in which opportunities for rest and resupply become the priority.

This book commences in Northern California, at the start of Section 7, where the PCT first crosses Interstate 5, not too far from Mount Shasta, continuing to the second crossing of Interstate 5, close to Ashland. At this point the trail has crossed into Oregon and Sections 8 and 9 take the hiker as far as the Washington border at Cascade Locks, breaking at McKenzie Pass, a short hop from the town of Sisters. Finally, Sections 10 and 11 cross Washington, breaking at Snoqualmie Pass before finally reaching the Northern Terminus at the border with Canada.

Hikers ascending a ridge as a storm threatens overhead (Stage 60)

USING THIS GUIDE

This, book three of the guide, is intended to be used by the hiker who has first read book one, *Hiking the Pacific Crest Trail*. There you will find a more detailed explanation of the trail structure, history, timings, permits required, navigation and how to approach a hike on the PCT, whether a thru-hike or a shorter section.

The route maps are presented at 1:100,000 scale, sufficient to navigate from topography and major features most of the time. Smaller details that might be required to navigate in poor conditions will not be present. Mapping is continuous throughout each booklet, and mileage is given cumulatively from 0–2655. Stage timings are indicative only, and do not include breaks. Individuals will hike faster or slower than the suggested timings. The water sources indicated can vary greatly from year to year. Many will dry up during the season, earlier some years than others. Water caches are indicated where commonly seen, but should never be relied upon.

The PCT Water Report is an invaluable crowd-sourced project managed by volunteers. It provides updates regarding water sources, fires, passes, and fords. You can access it at www.pctwater.com, on Instagram @pctwater, or on Facebook. You can also download it in several formats for offline use. Please contribute updates whenever you can.

SECTION 7 – INTERSTATE 5 (CASTELLA) TO INTERSTATE 5 (ASHLAND)

Stage		Distance (miles)	Total ascent (feet)	Total descent (feet)	Duration (hr:min)	Page
56	I-5 (Castella) – Parks Creek Rd	38.5	7165	2451	19:00	17
57	Parks Creek Rd – Hwy 3	20.5	886	2372	8:00	19
58	Hwy 3 – Carter Meadows Summit	19.8	3077	2283	9:10	21
59	Carter Meadows Summit – Etna Summit	19.7	3789	4019	9:50	23
60	Etna Summit – Paradise Lake	29.1	5387	5223	13:55	25
61	Paradise Lake – Seiad Valley	27.1	1886	6706	10:00	26
62	Seiad Valley – Cook and Green Pass	14.8	5157	1762	9:35	28
63	Cook and Green Pass – Wrangle Gap	27.6	4954	3228	13:00	30
64	Wrangle Gap – I-5 (Ashland)	20.4	1831	4062	8:30	34
Totals		**217.5**	**34,132**	**32,106**	**101:00**	

WHAT TO EXPECT

Section 7 holds a bit of a surprise for the hiker that arrives here as part of a longer hike. There is a break in the volcanic nature of the land around the trail you've been following and, like the Sierra Nevada, here granite is the primary underlying rock. The similarities do not end there. With granite supporting moisture more readily the area is rich in lakes, although sadly the PCT route visits only three. That is largely because the PCT remains on the crest where many lakes are situated in deep basins that hold snow late into summer. The trail on the other hand hugs south and west facing slopes and should be largely snow-free by mid July.

It is here that the trail snakes west as part of a large arc around three sides of Mount Shasta. Part of the Klamath Mountains, the trail passes through the Trinity Alps, Russian and Marble Mountain Wilderness areas before turning back east and heading at decreasing altitudes to the Oregon border. The descent into Seiad Valley holds one of the less celebrated records of the PCT, that of the longest road walk. There has long been talk of the potential for a new bridge across the Klamath River to straighten

MEDFORD
Ashland
Upper Klamath Lake
KLAMATH FALLS
Interstate 5
63
64
62
Seiad Valley
Crescent City
61
Yreka
N
60
Etna
57
0 25 50 km
0 25 miles
Mount Shasta
59
58
Castella
56
Burney
EUREKA

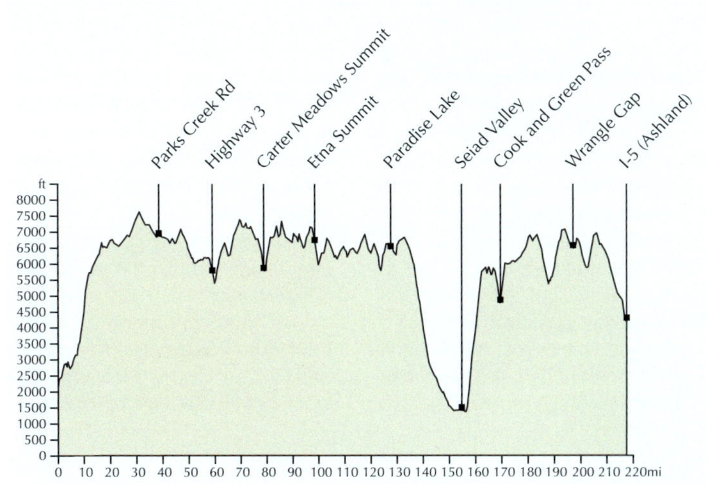
Parks Creek Rd
Highway 3
Carter Meadows Summit
Etna Summit
Paradise Lake
Seiad Valley
Cook and Green Pass
Wrangle Gap
I-5 (Ashland)
ft
8000
7500
7000
6500
6000
5500
5000
4500
4000
3500
3000
2500
2000
1500
1000
500
0
0 10 20 30 40 50 60 70 80 90 100 110 120 130 140 150 160 170 180 190 200 210 220mi

the line of the trail and reduce the extent of paved road that is necessary to walk, but there appears to be little inclination to overcome the financial and logistical challenges required to achieve this.

Unsurprisingly, with the trail hugging high ridges as much as possible, water sources can be limited and many dry out within weeks of the snow melt, so care is again required here with managing limited water. The best times to hike are July to October when the trail is snow free. This would be a difficult section while snow remains.

This relatively short section is punctuated effectively by the highway at Etna Summit, where a growing group of trail angels make hitching down to the small mountain town of Etna much easier. This is particularly helpful as there isn't much in the way of resupply options before or after. Etna's mid-sized markets and an outdoor gear retailer make for an effective and worthwhile stop, and donation-based camping in the town park, complete with a basic shower, help to keep costs to a minimum. Beyond this there is the general store at Seiad Valley which is making an effort to cater to hikers, but at peak season their stock runs perilously low.

Crossing the border into Oregon is a milestone to be celebrated after 1700 miles of California. It also provides the opportunity to visit a city with all the requisite resources and pleasures. Callahan's Lodge, close to the trail has long been the convenient staging post for a foray into the city, but increasingly new services to hikers are opening up in Ashland itself, including some affordable lodging. The hitch in can be a pain, but if you are feeling adventurous consider the proposed alternate that takes a side trail directly to join one end of Ashland city park.

PERMITS

Permits are required for overnight trips in Trinity Alps Wilderness, PCT miles 1564.0 to 1581.1.

These are free and available at outdoor 'kiosks' located at the Weaverville Ranger Station (360 Main St), at the kiosk outside of the Supervisor's Office in Redding (3644 Avtech Parkway), at the Shasta Lake Ranger Station (14225 Holiday Road), and at the Fire Stations (Mule Creek and Coffee Creek off Highway 3 and Junction City and Big Bar off Highway 299).

For ease, hikers may want to consider hiking through the permit area without camping.

For more information call the Trinity Alps Wilderness office at (530) 623-2121 or visit: www.fs.usda.gov/recarea/stnf/recarea/?recid=6521.

RESUPPLY OPTIONS

Stage	Trail mile	Place	Off trail (miles)	Description	Facilities
59	1600.7	Etna	10.4 NE	Friendly rural town, camping in park, outfitters, good resupply	
61	1656.9	Seiad Valley	On trail	Small community, great diner,	
61	1656.9	Seiad Valley	On trail	Wildwood Tavern and Lodge 0.5mi W of PO offers camping, food and showers	
64	1719.7	Callahan's Lodge	0.8 N	Lodge with dedicated camping and facilities, accepts packages ($)	
64	1719.7	Ashland	13.0 NW	Large town, full facilities, hospital, good outfitter	

MAIL DROP INFORMATION

Callahan's Mountain Lodge
'Your Name Here'
c/o Callahan's PCT Hiker
7100 Old Hwy 99 S,
Ashland, OR 97520
ETA: 'Your ETA'
They are open: Mon–Sun 7am–9pm
Phone them on: (541) 482-1299
Visit them at: www.callahanslodge.com

POST OFFICE INFORMATION

'Your Name Here'
c\o General Delivery
Etna, CA 96027
Located at: 119 Diggles Street
Phone them on: (530) 467-3981

'Your Name Here'
c\o General Delivery
Seiad Valley, CA 96086
Located at: 44717 State Highway 96
Phone them on: (530) 496-3211

'Your Name Here'
c\o General Delivery
Ashland, OR 97520
Located at: 120 N 1st Street
Phone them on: (541) 552-1622

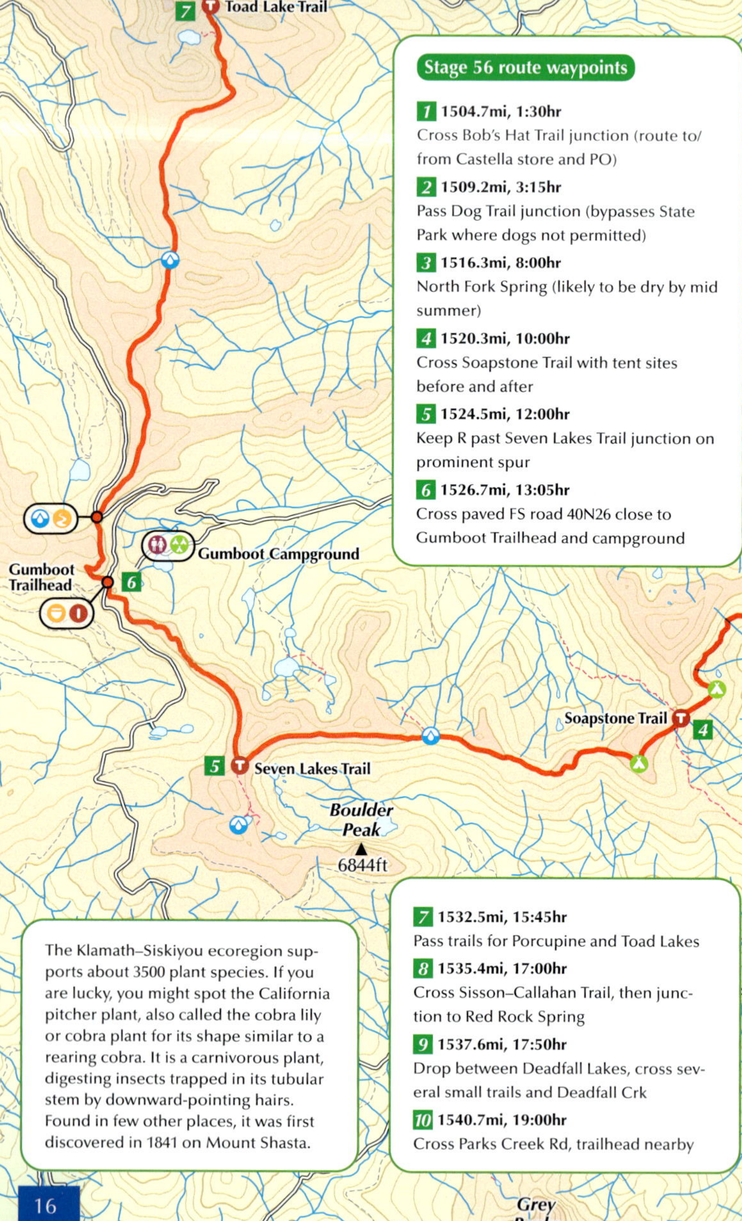

Stage 56 route waypoints

1 1504.7mi, 1:30hr
Cross Bob's Hat Trail junction (route to/from Castella store and PO)

2 1509.2mi, 3:15hr
Pass Dog Trail junction (bypasses State Park where dogs not permitted)

3 1516.3mi, 8:00hr
North Fork Spring (likely to be dry by mid summer)

4 1520.3mi, 10:00hr
Cross Soapstone Trail with tent sites before and after

5 1524.5mi, 12:00hr
Keep R past Seven Lakes Trail junction on prominent spur

6 1526.7mi, 13:05hr
Cross paved FS road 40N26 close to Gumboot Trailhead and campground

7 1532.5mi, 15:45hr
Pass trails for Porcupine and Toad Lakes

8 1535.4mi, 17:00hr
Cross Sisson–Callahan Trail, then junction to Red Rock Spring

9 1537.6mi, 17:50hr
Drop between Deadfall Lakes, cross several small trails and Deadfall Crk

10 1540.7mi, 19:00hr
Cross Parks Creek Rd, trailhead nearby

The Klamath–Siskiyou ecoregion supports about 3500 plant species. If you are lucky, you might spot the California pitcher plant, also called the cobra lily or cobra plant for its shape similar to a rearing cobra. It is a carnivorous plant, digesting insects trapped in its tubular stem by downward-pointing hairs. Found in few other places, it was first discovered in 1841 on Mount Shasta.

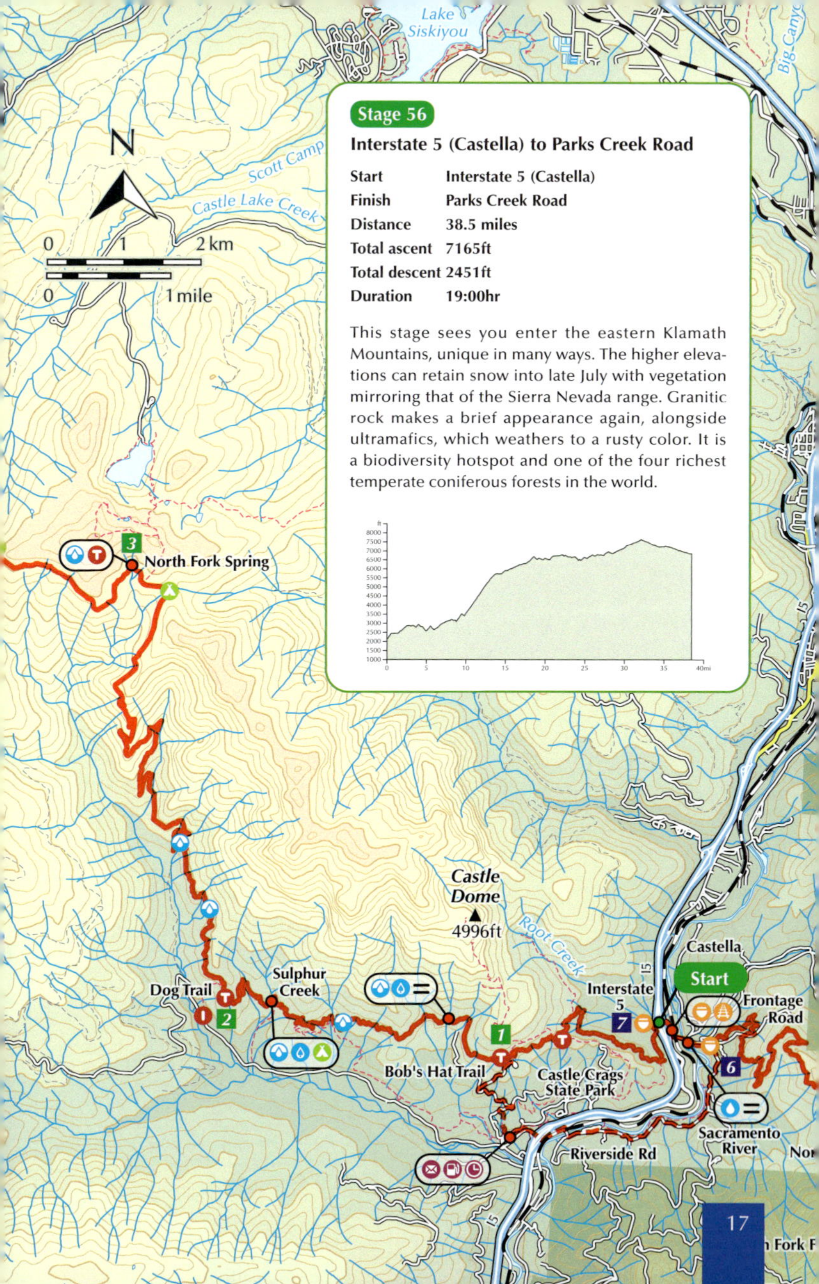

Stage 56

Interstate 5 (Castella) to Parks Creek Road

Start	**Interstate 5 (Castella)**
Finish	**Parks Creek Road**
Distance	**38.5 miles**
Total ascent	**7165ft**
Total descent	**2451ft**
Duration	**19:00hr**

This stage sees you enter the eastern Klamath Mountains, unique in many ways. The higher elevations can retain snow into late July with vegetation mirroring that of the Sierra Nevada range. Granitic rock makes a brief appearance again, alongside ultramafics, which weathers to a rusty color. It is a biodiversity hotspot and one of the four richest temperate coniferous forests in the world.

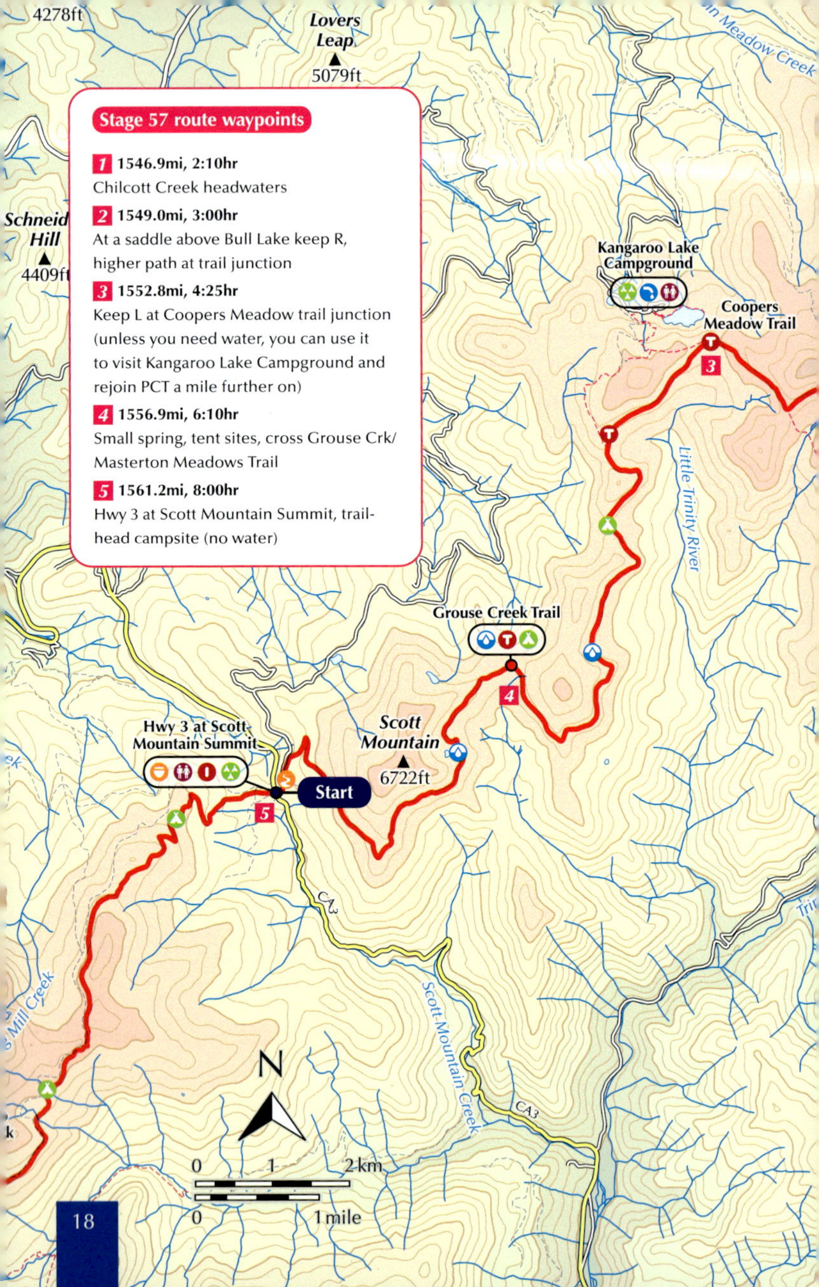
Stage 57 route waypoints
1 1546.9mi, 2:10hr
Chilcott Creek headwaters
2 1549.0mi, 3:00hr
At a saddle above Bull Lake keep R, higher path at trail junction
3 1552.8mi, 4:25hr
Keep L at Coopers Meadow trail junction (unless you need water, you can use it to visit Kangaroo Lake Campground and rejoin PCT a mile further on)
4 1556.9mi, 6:10hr
Small spring, tent sites, cross Grouse Crk/ Masterton Meadows Trail
5 1561.2mi, 8:00hr
Hwy 3 at Scott Mountain Summit, trail-head campsite (no water)
4278ft
Lovers Leap
5079ft
Schneid Hill
4409ft
Kangaroo Lake Campground
Coopers Meadow Trail
Little Trinity River
Grouse Creek Trail
Scott Mountain
6722ft
Hwy 3 at Scott Mountain Summit
Start
CA3
Scott Mountain Creek
Mill Creek
N
0
1
2 km
0
1 mile

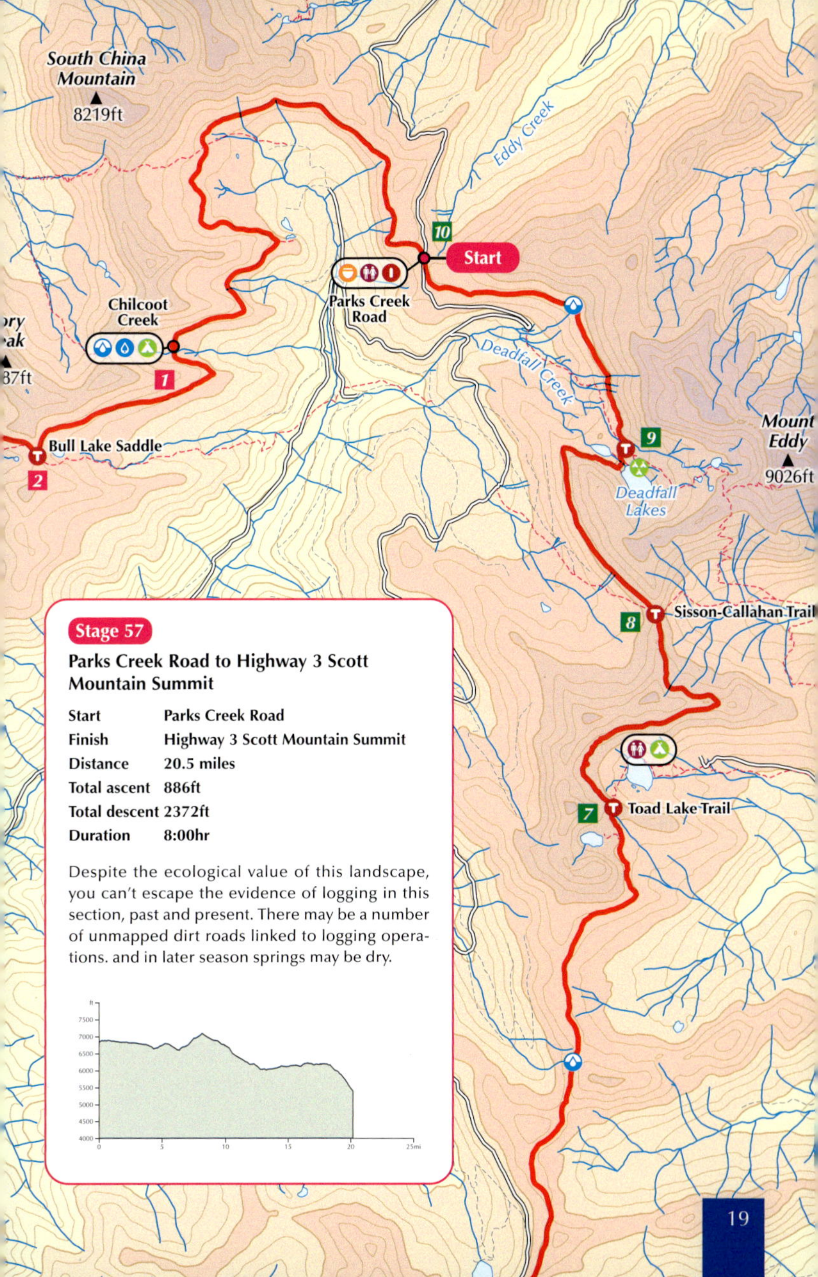

Stage 57

Parks Creek Road to Highway 3 Scott Mountain Summit

Start	**Parks Creek Road**
Finish	**Highway 3 Scott Mountain Summit**
Distance	**20.5 miles**
Total ascent	**886ft**
Total descent	**2372ft**
Duration	**8:00hr**

Despite the ecological value of this landscape, you can't escape the evidence of logging in this section, past and present. There may be a number of unmapped dirt roads linked to logging operations. and in later season springs may be dry.

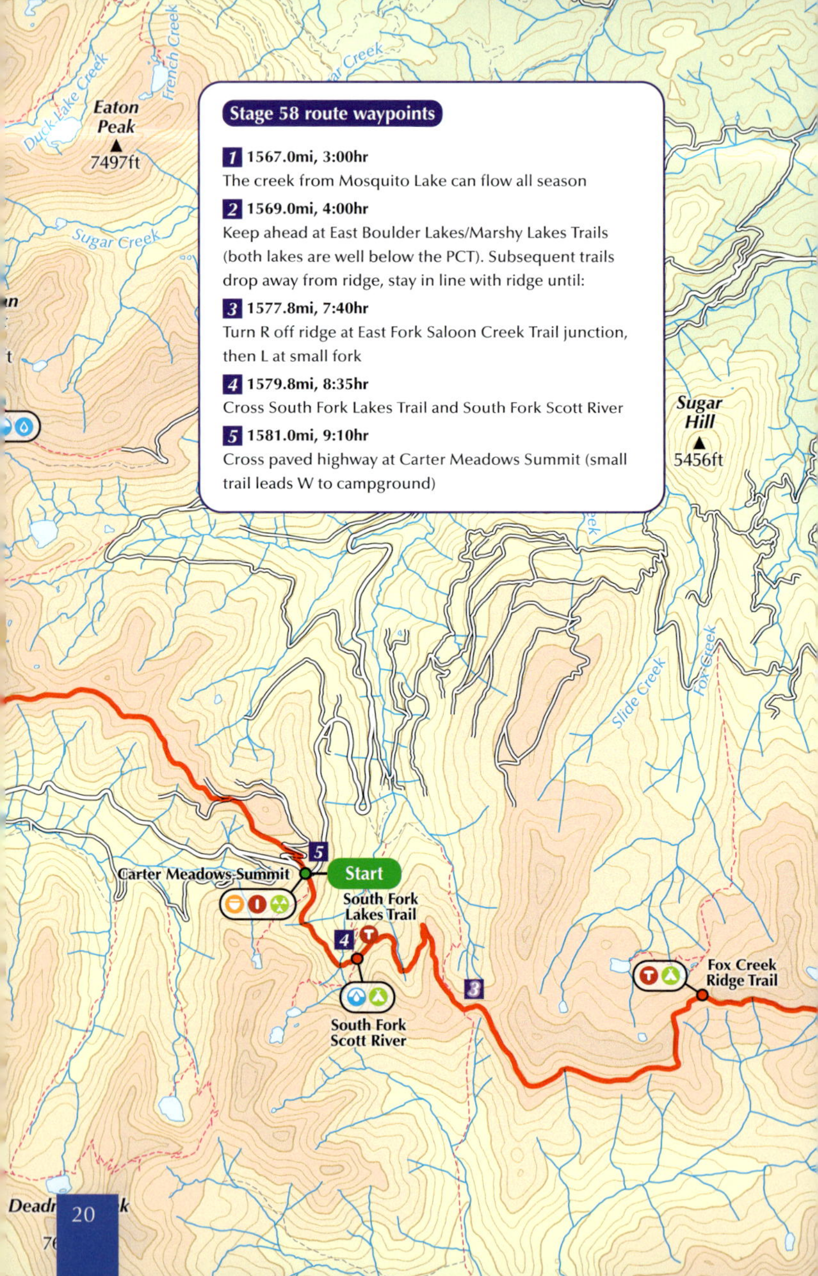

Stage 58 route waypoints
1 1567.0mi, 3:00hr
The creek from Mosquito Lake can flow all season
2 1569.0mi, 4:00hr
Keep ahead at East Boulder Lakes/Marshy Lakes Trails (both lakes are well below the PCT). Subsequent trails drop away from ridge, stay in line with ridge until:
3 1577.8mi, 7:40hr
Turn R off ridge at East Fork Saloon Creek Trail junction, then L at small fork
4 1579.8mi, 8:35hr
Cross South Fork Lakes Trail and South Fork Scott River
5 1581.0mi, 9:10hr
Cross paved highway at Carter Meadows Summit (small trail leads W to campground)
Duck Lake Creek
French Creek
Eaton Peak
7497ft
Sugar Creek
Sugar Hill
5456ft
Slide Creek
Fox Creek
Carter Meadows Summit
5
Start
South Fork Lakes Trail
4
South Fork Scott River
3
Fox Creek Ridge Trail

Stage 58

Highway 3 Scott Mountain Summit to Carter Meadows Summit

Start	**Highway 3 Scott Mountain Summit**
Finish	**Carter Meadows Summit**
Distance	**19.8 miles**
Total ascent	**3077ft**
Total descent	**2283ft**
Duration	**9:10hr**

Leaving Scott Mountain, you face an initial 1200ft climb but at least have some shade. As you cross into the northern tip of Trinity Alps Wilderness the views really open up, including south to the Trinity River Valley and north to Mount Shasta.

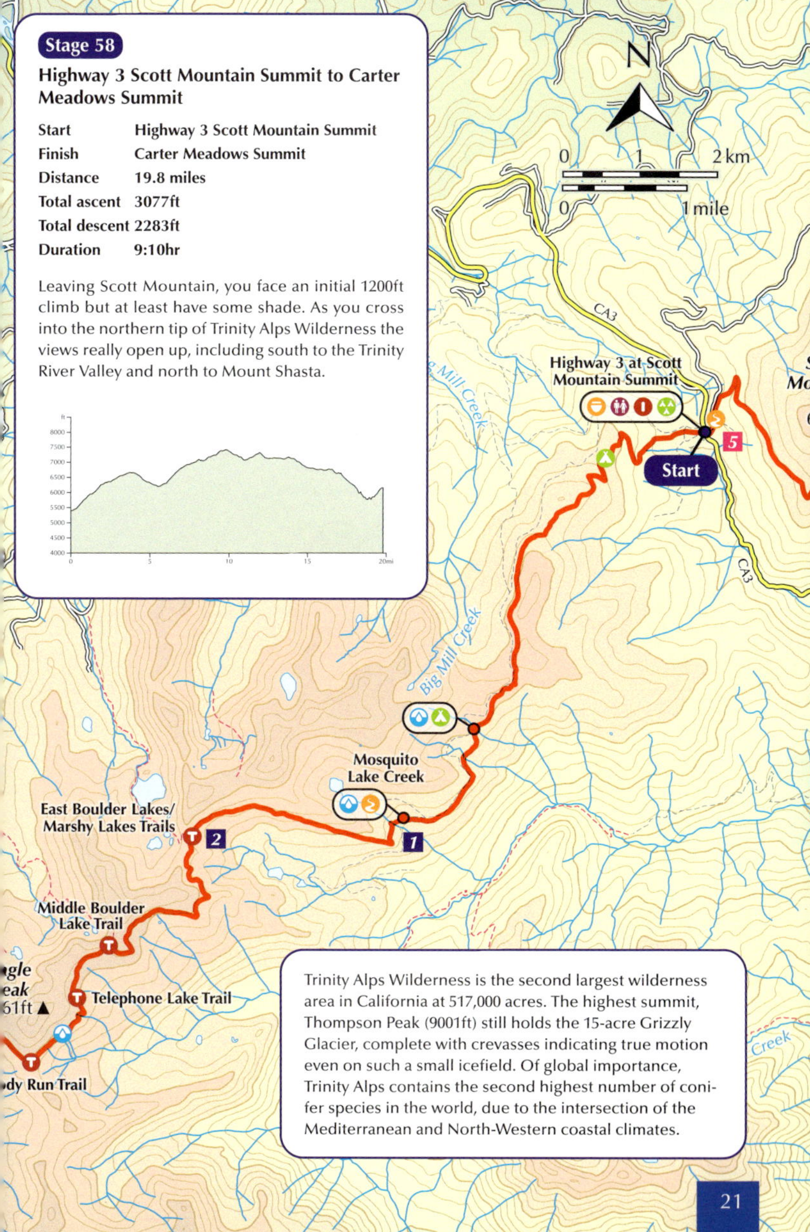

Trinity Alps Wilderness is the second largest wilderness area in California at 517,000 acres. The highest summit, Thompson Peak (9001ft) still holds the 15-acre Grizzly Glacier, complete with crevasses indicating true motion even on such a small icefield. Of global importance, Trinity Alps contains the second highest number of conifer species in the world, due to the intersection of the Mediterranean and North-Western coastal climates.

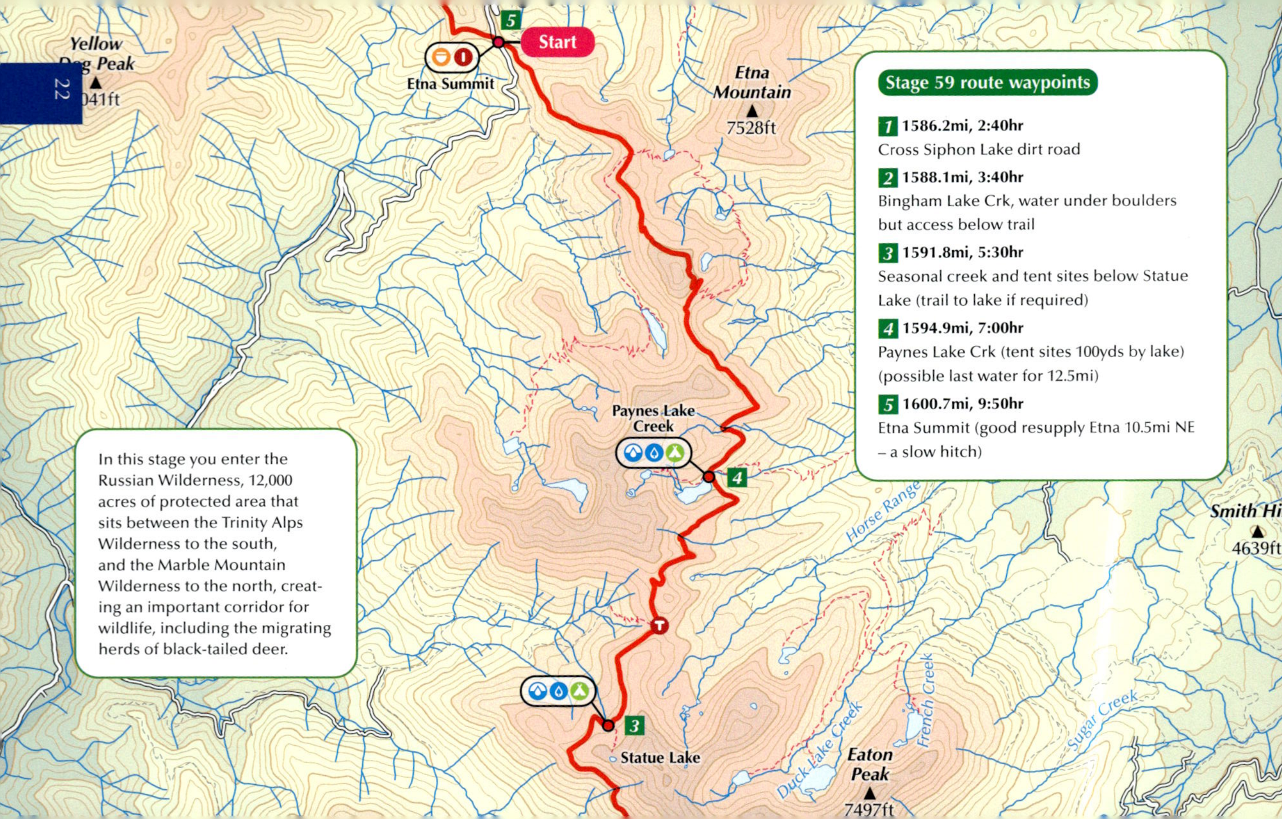

Stage 59 route waypoints

1 1586.2mi, 2:40hr
Cross Siphon Lake dirt road

2 1588.1mi, 3:40hr
Bingham Lake Crk, water under boulders but access below trail

3 1591.8mi, 5:30hr
Seasonal creek and tent sites below Statue Lake (trail to lake if required)

4 1594.9mi, 7:00hr
Paynes Lake Crk (tent sites 100yds by lake) (possible last water for 12.5mi)

5 1600.7mi, 9:50hr
Etna Summit (good resupply Etna 10.5mi NE – a slow hitch)

In this stage you enter the Russian Wilderness, 12,000 acres of protected area that sits between the Trinity Alps Wilderness to the south, and the Marble Mountain Wilderness to the north, creating an important corridor for wildlife, including the migrating herds of black-tailed deer.

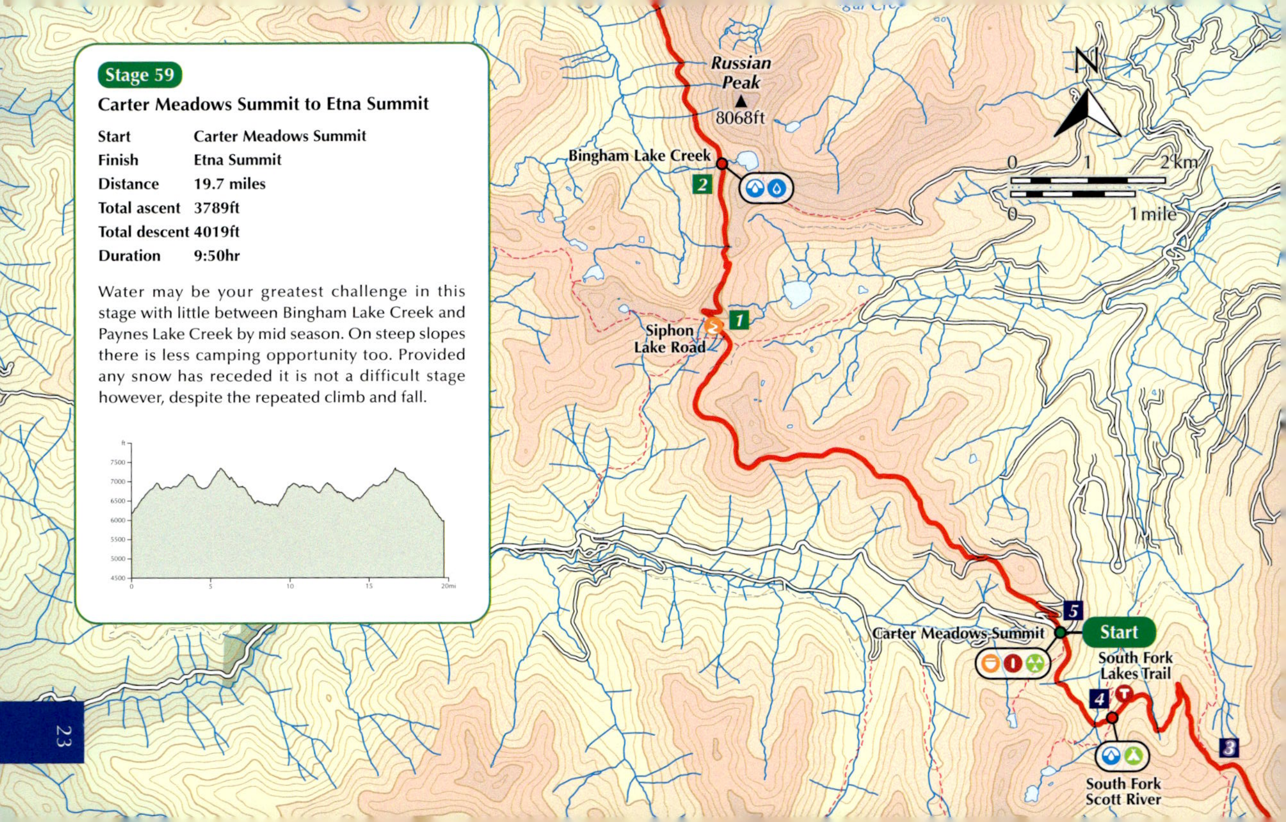

Stage 59

Carter Meadows Summit to Etna Summit

Start	Carter Meadows Summit
Finish	Etna Summit
Distance	19.7 miles
Total ascent	3789ft
Total descent	4019ft
Duration	9:50hr

Water may be your greatest challenge in this stage with little between Bingham Lake Creek and Paynes Lake Creek by mid season. On steep slopes there is less camping opportunity too. Provided any snow has receded it is not a difficult stage however, despite the repeated climb and fall.

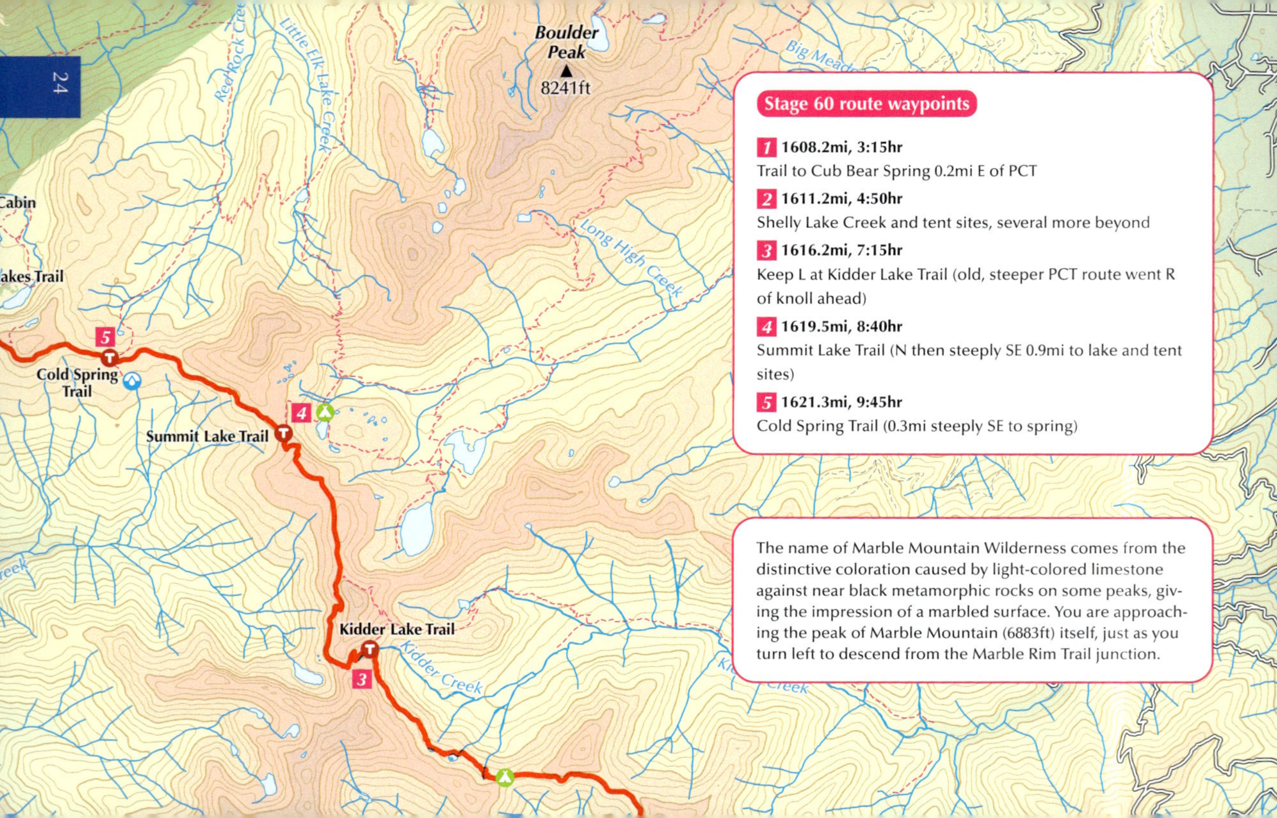

Stage 60 route waypoints

1 1608.2mi, 3:15hr
Trail to Cub Bear Spring 0.2mi E of PCT

2 1611.2mi, 4:50hr
Shelly Lake Creek and tent sites, several more beyond

3 1616.2mi, 7:15hr
Keep L at Kidder Lake Trail (old, steeper PCT route went R of knoll ahead)

4 1619.5mi, 8:40hr
Summit Lake Trail (N then steeply SE 0.9mi to lake and tent sites)

5 1621.3mi, 9:45hr
Cold Spring Trail (0.3mi steeply SE to spring)

The name of Marble Mountain Wilderness comes from the distinctive coloration caused by light-colored limestone against near black metamorphic rocks on some peaks, giving the impression of a marbled surface. You are approaching the peak of Marble Mountain (6883ft) itself, just as you turn left to descend from the Marble Rim Trail junction.

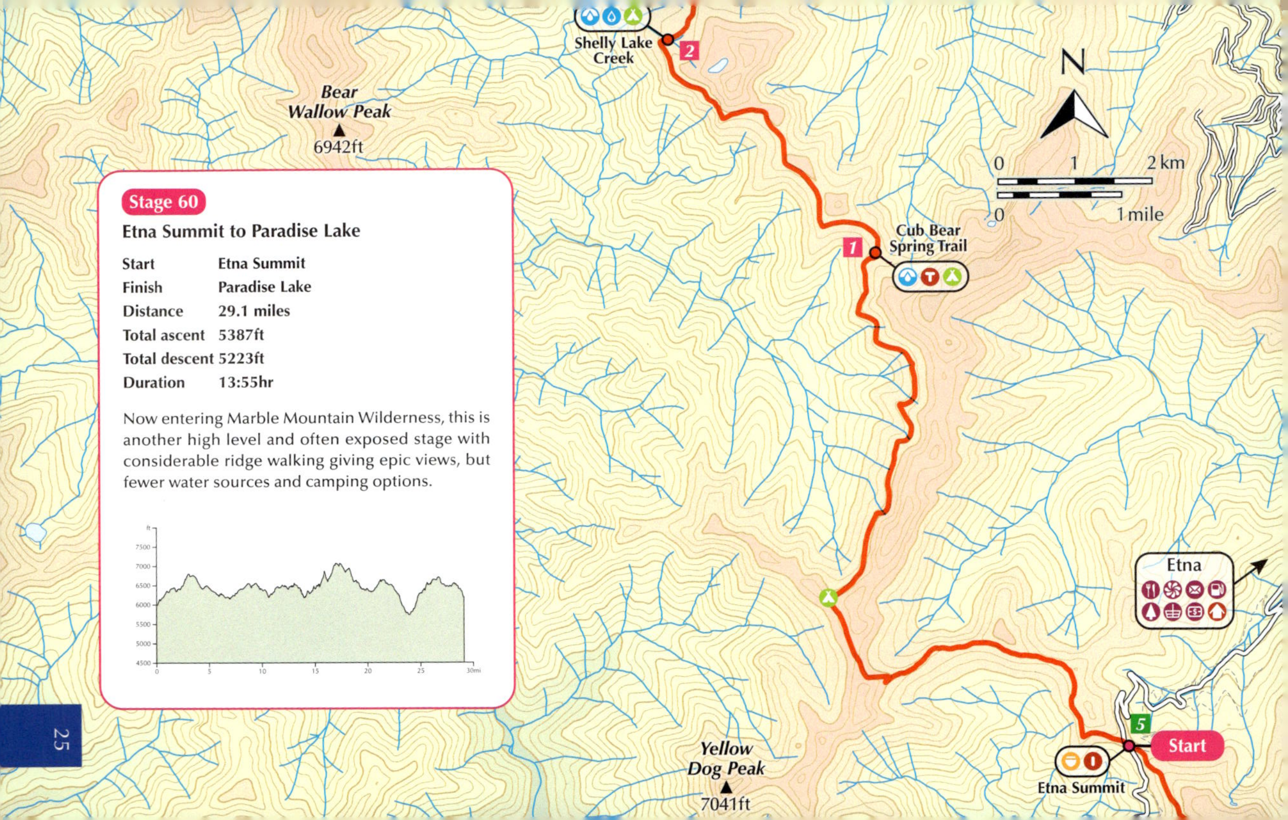

Stage 60

Etna Summit to Paradise Lake

Start	**Etna Summit**
Finish	**Paradise Lake**
Distance	**29.1 miles**
Total ascent	**5387ft**
Total descent	**5223ft**
Duration	**13:55hr**

Now entering Marble Mountain Wilderness, this is another high level and often exposed stage with considerable ridge walking giving epic views, but fewer water sources and camping options.

Stage 61

Paradise Lake to Seiad Valley

Start	**Paradise Lake**
Finish	**Seiad Valley**
Distance	**27.1 miles**
Total ascent	**1886ft**
Total descent	**6706ft**
Duration	**10:00hr**

This stage holds the dubious title of including the longest road walk on the PCT. At 6.4 miles, the walk from Grider Creek campground into Seiad Valley can seem endless. However, walk gently and don't rush it. Walking on paved road can be hard on your feet after weeks on trails. More than a few hikers have arrived in Seiad Valley with new blisters or worse, strain injuries, from this road walk.

Stage 61 route waypoints

1 1635.5mi, 2:15hr
Buckthorn Spring Trail (150ft W, in meadow, under three-forked tree)

2 1642.5mi, 5:10hr
Ford Cold Spring Crk, a large creek, followed by four bridge crossings of Grider Crk

Stage 60 route waypoints – continued
6 1623.7mi, 10:50hr
Take R off ridge at Marble Rim Trail junction
7 1624.6mi, 11:15hr
Creek near Marble Valley Cabin (locked), Canyon Creek Trail junction
8 1629.8mi, 13:55hr
Paradise Lake, junction E to Paradise Trailhead
Turk Lake Trail
Kings Castle
7405ft
Start
Paradise Lake
Paradise Lake Trailhead
South Fork Kelsey Creek
Box Camp Mountain
7267ft
Elk Creek
Box Camp Trail
Black Marble Mountain
7434ft
Toms Valley Creek
Rainy Valley Creek
Elk Peak
6929ft
Marble Mountain
6883ft
Marble Valley Cabin
Marble Rim Trail
Sky High Lakes Trail
Cold Spring Trail
Red Rock Creek
Pigeon Roost
6424ft
N
0
1
2 km
1 mile

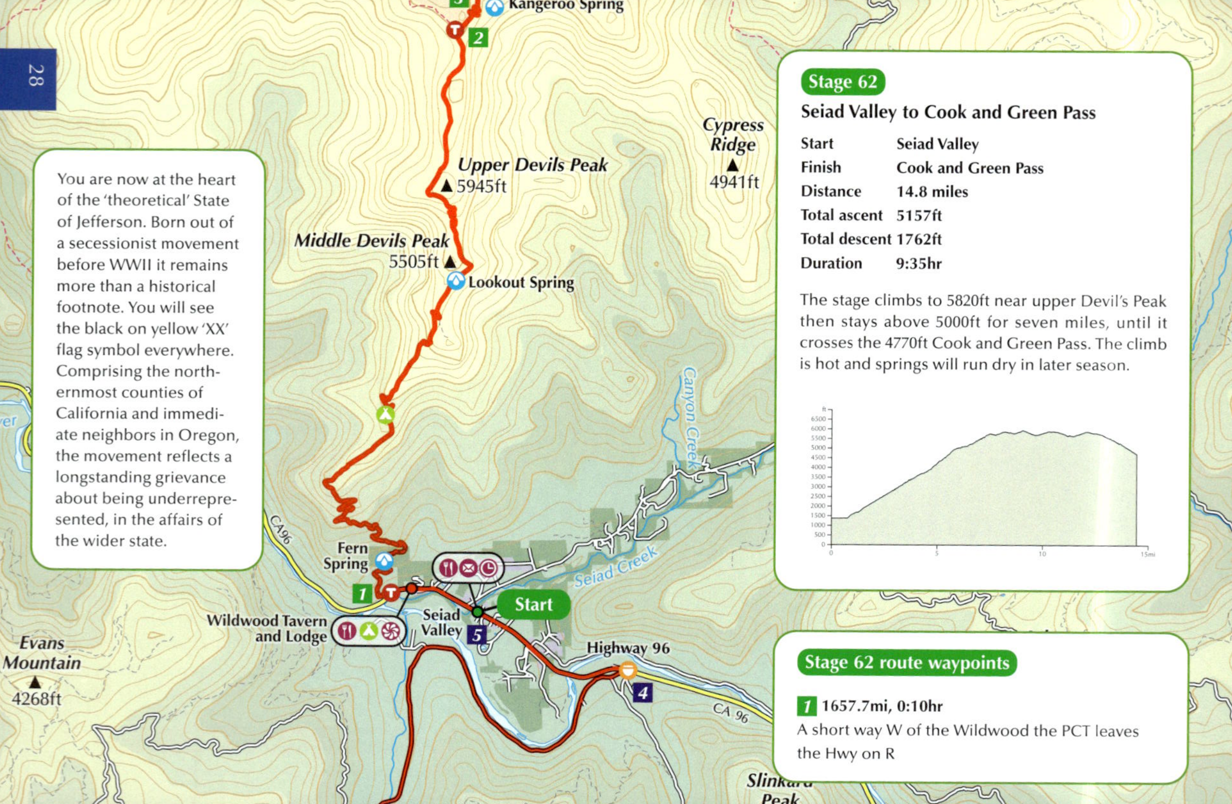

You are now at the heart of the 'theoretical' State of Jefferson. Born out of a secessionist movement before WWII it remains more than a historical footnote. You will see the black on yellow 'XX' flag symbol everywhere. Comprising the northernmost counties of California and immediate neighbors in Oregon, the movement reflects a longstanding grievance about being underrepresented, in the affairs of the wider state.

Stage 62

Seiad Valley to Cook and Green Pass

Start	**Seiad Valley**
Finish	**Cook and Green Pass**
Distance	**14.8 miles**
Total ascent	**5157ft**
Total descent	**1762ft**
Duration	**9:35hr**

The stage climbs to 5820ft near upper Devil's Peak then stays above 5000ft for seven miles, until it crosses the 4770ft Cook and Green Pass. The climb is hot and springs will run dry in later season.

Stage 62 route waypoints

1 1657.7mi, 0:10hr
A short way W of the Wildwood the PCT leaves the Hwy on R

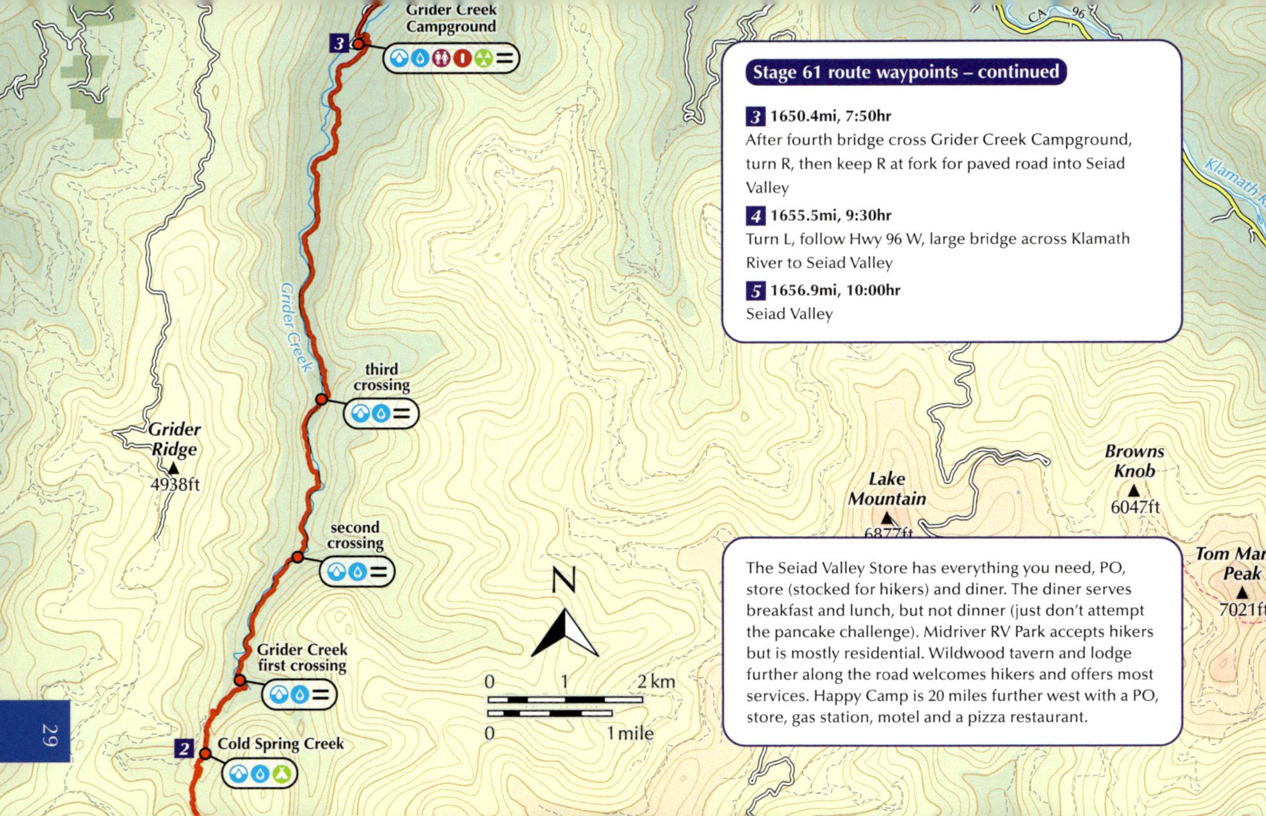

Stage 61 route waypoints – continued

3 1650.4mi, 7:50hr
After fourth bridge cross Grider Creek Campground, turn R, then keep R at fork for paved road into Seiad Valley

4 1655.5mi, 9:30hr
Turn L, follow Hwy 96 W, large bridge across Klamath River to Seiad Valley

5 1656.9mi, 10:00hr
Seiad Valley

The Seiad Valley Store has everything you need, PO, store (stocked for hikers) and diner. The diner serves breakfast and lunch, but not dinner (just don't attempt the pancake challenge). Midriver RV Park accepts hikers but is mostly residential. Wildwood tavern and lodge further along the road welcomes hikers and offers most services. Happy Camp is 20 miles further west with a PO, store, gas station, motel and a pizza restaurant.

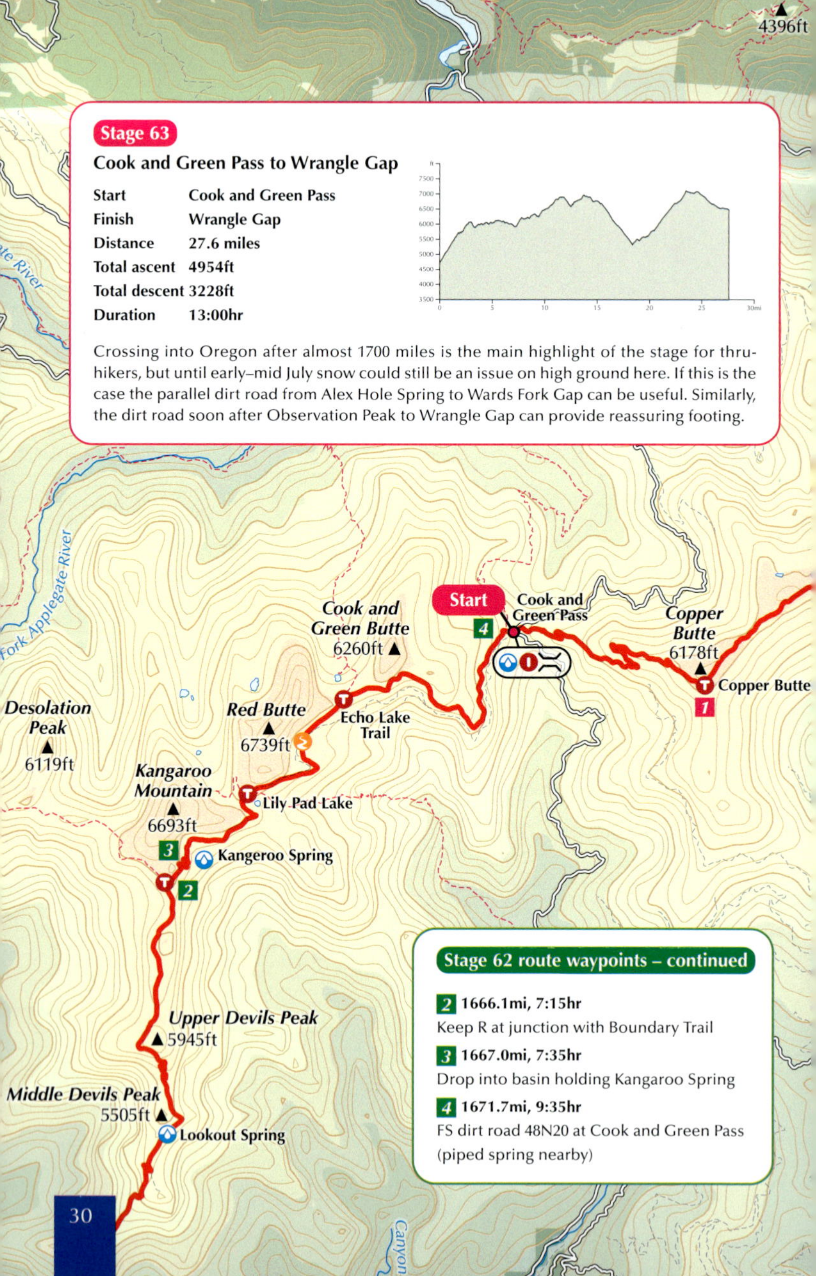

Stage 63
Cook and Green Pass to Wrangle Gap
Start Cook and Green Pass
Finish Wrangle Gap
Distance 27.6 miles
Total ascent 4954ft
Total descent 3228ft
Duration 13:00hr
ft
7500
7000
6500
6000
5500
5000
4500
4000
3500
0
5
10
15
20
25
30mi
Crossing into Oregon after almost 1700 miles is the main highlight of the stage for thru-hikers, but until early–mid July snow could still be an issue on high ground here. If this is the case the parallel dirt road from Alex Hole Spring to Wards Fork Gap can be useful. Similarly, the dirt road soon after Observation Peak to Wrangle Gap can provide reassuring footing.
4396ft
Fork Applegate River
Start
Cook and Green Pass
4
Copper Butte 6178ft
Copper Butte
1
Cook and Green Butte 6260ft
Echo Lake Trail
Red Butte 6739ft
Desolation Peak 6119ft
Kangaroo Mountain 6693ft
Lily Pad Lake
3
Kangeroo Spring
2
Upper Devils Peak 5945ft
Middle Devils Peak 5505ft
Lookout Spring
Canyon
Stage 62 route waypoints – continued
2 1666.1mi, 7:15hr
Keep R at junction with Boundary Trail
3 1667.0mi, 7:35hr
Drop into basin holding Kangaroo Spring
4 1671.7mi, 9:35hr
FS dirt road 48N20 at Cook and Green Pass (piped spring nearby)

Stage 63 route waypoints
1 1674.5mi, 2:00hr
Keep L at Copper Butte Trail
2 1677.1mi, 3:00hr
Bear Dog Spring side of trail – S
3 1684.2mi, 6:10hr
Alex Hole Spring side of trail – N
Scraggy Mountain
6946ft
Mud Spring
Black Mountain
6375ft
Dog
ring
Condrey Mountain
7100ft
Alex Hole Spring
N
0
1
2 km
0
1 mile
White Cloud Mountain
4213ft

Acorn Woman Mountain
5164ft
Just 0.5 miles west of Wrangle Gap is Wrangle Campground. A lightly used camp due to its remote location, this is especially worth a visit in poor weather for the 'community kitchen' a fabulous shelter built during the Great Depression (1935–36) by the Civilian Conservation Corps (CCC). With benches and beams to hang wet gear from this could be a great place to dry out.
Dutchman Peak
7415ft
Sheep Camp Spring
Yellowjacket Mountain
6295ft
7339ft
Observation Peak
Donomore Peak
6617ft
7
California–Oregon borde
Donomore Creek and Cabin
6
Wards Fork Gap
5
4
Bearground Spring
Scraggy
6946ft
Mud Spring
Condrey Mountain
7100ft
3
Alex Hole Spring

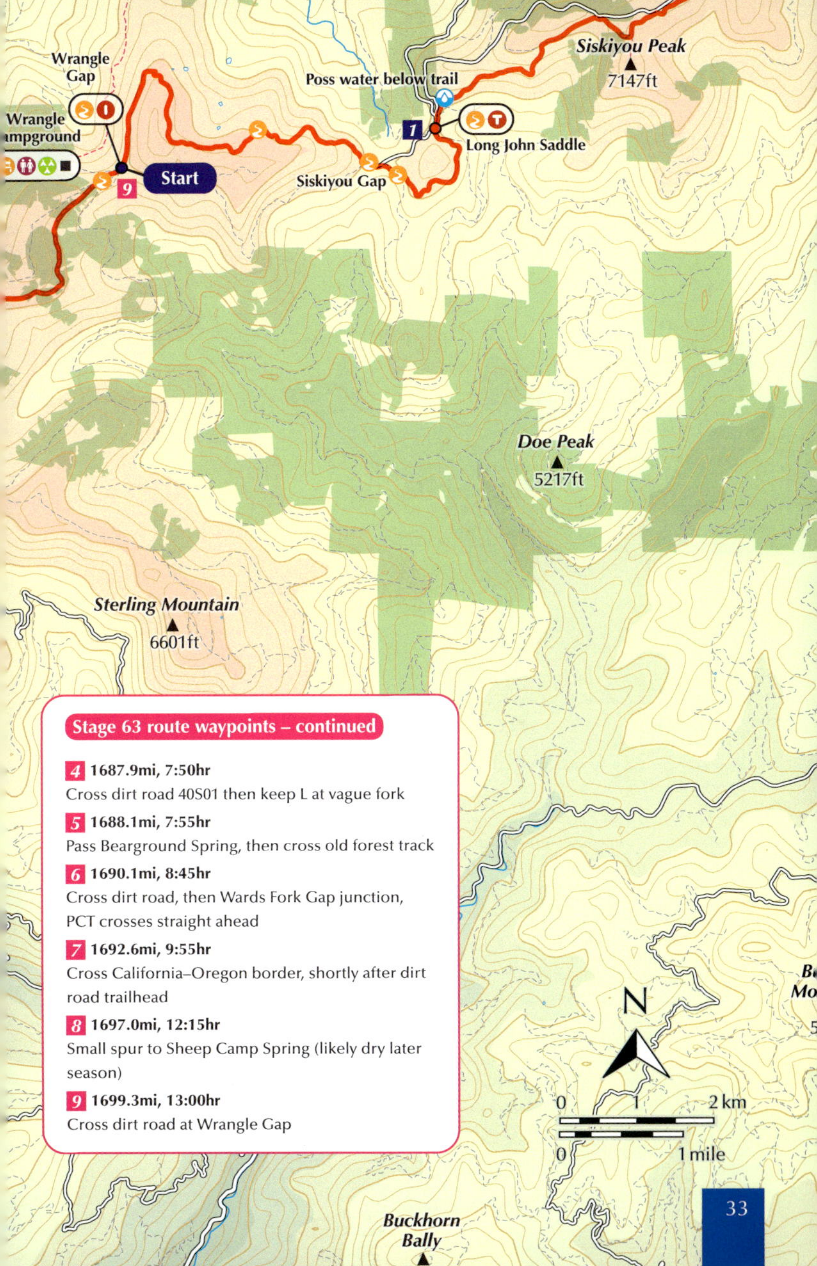

Stage 63 route waypoints – continued

4 1687.9mi, 7:50hr
Cross dirt road 40S01 then keep L at vague fork

5 1688.1mi, 7:55hr
Pass Bearground Spring, then cross old forest track

6 1690.1mi, 8:45hr
Cross dirt road, then Wards Fork Gap junction, PCT crosses straight ahead

7 1692.6mi, 9:55hr
Cross California–Oregon border, shortly after dirt road trailhead

8 1697.0mi, 12:15hr
Small spur to Sheep Camp Spring (likely dry later season)

9 1699.3mi, 13:00hr
Cross dirt road at Wrangle Gap

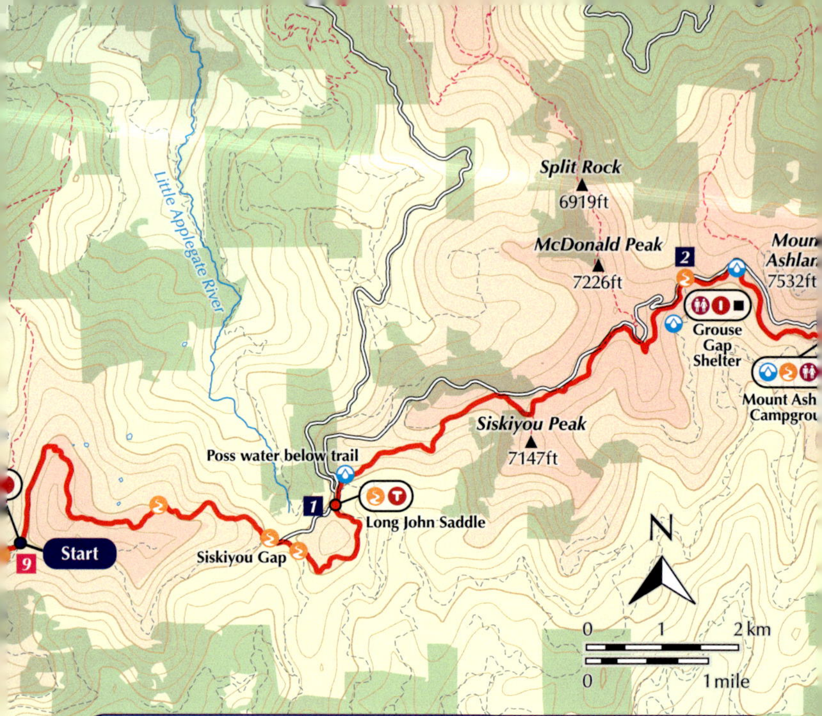

Split Rock
6919ft
McDonald Peak
7226ft
2
Mount Ashland
7532ft
Grouse Gap Shelter
Mount Ash Campgrou
Little Applegate River
Siskiyou Peak
7147ft
Poss water below trail
1
Long John Saddle
Start
9
Siskiyou Gap
N
0 1 2 km
0 1 mile
erling M
6601

Stage 64

Wrangle Gap to Interstate 5 (Ashland)

Start	**Wrangle Gap**
Finish	**Interstate 5 (Ashland)**
Distance	**20.4 miles**
Total ascent	**1831ft**
Total descent	**4062ft**
Duration	**8:30hr**

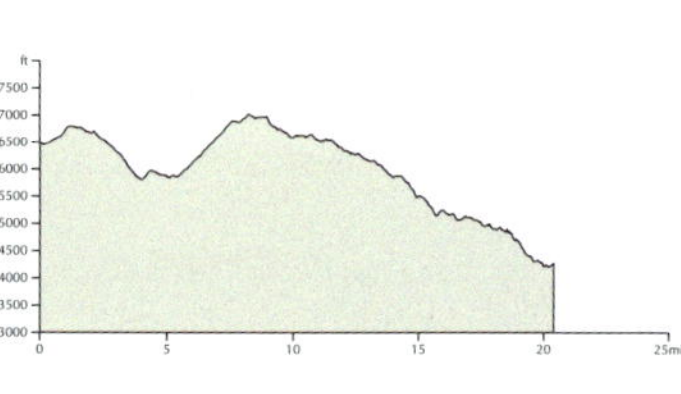

There is no reliable water on trail in this stage as you descend to Interstate 5 south of Ashland where most will resupply and perhaps enjoy some town comforts. As an alternative to hitching the 13 miles into Ashland from the trail crossing, consider taking the Bull Gap Trail from just beyond Mount Ashland, 12 miles via Coggins Saddle and Lambs Saddle, to the lower reservoir in Ashland's Lithia Park (where there is a water fountain), then 1.5 miles further to the heart of Ashland.

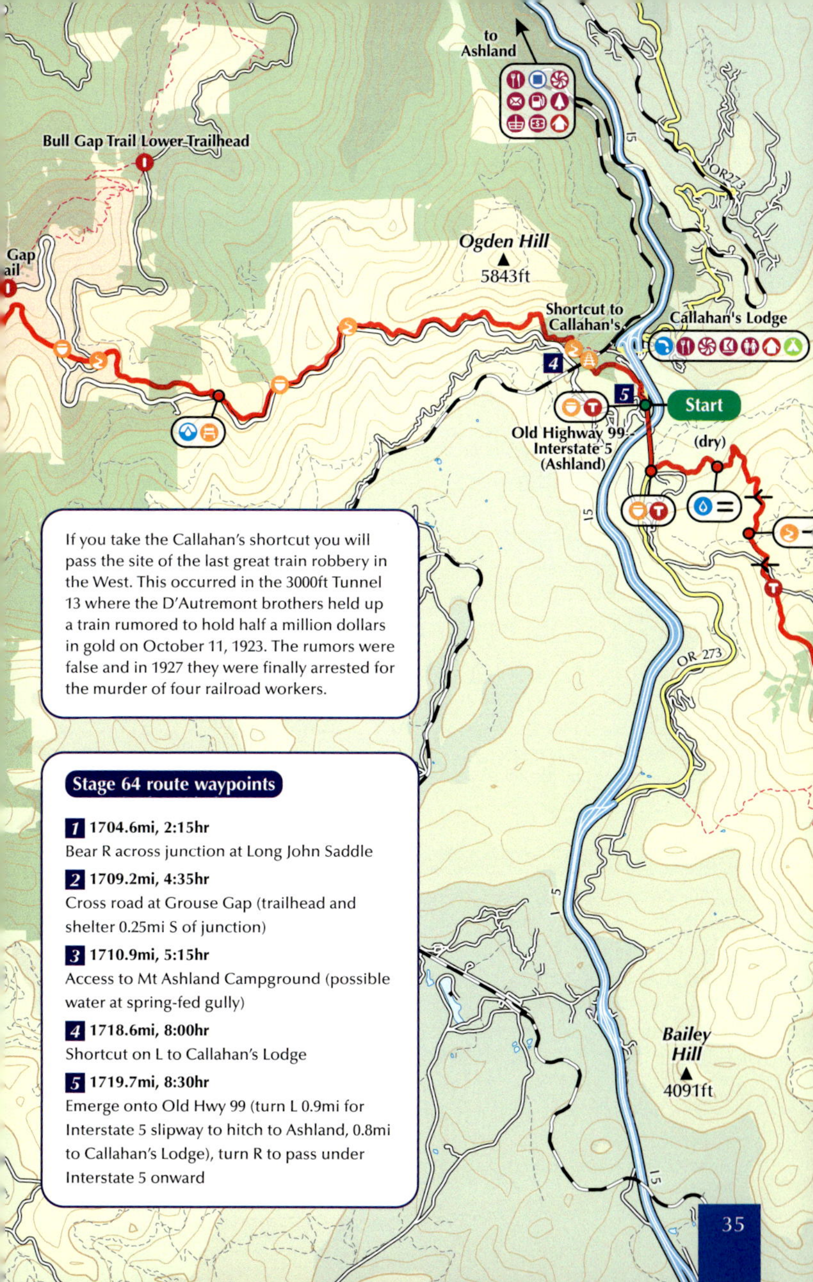

If you take the Callahan's shortcut you will pass the site of the last great train robbery in the West. This occurred in the 3000ft Tunnel 13 where the D'Autremont brothers held up a train rumored to hold half a million dollars in gold on October 11, 1923. The rumors were false and in 1927 they were finally arrested for the murder of four railroad workers.

Stage 64 route waypoints

1 1704.6mi, 2:15hr
Bear R across junction at Long John Saddle

2 1709.2mi, 4:35hr
Cross road at Grouse Gap (trailhead and shelter 0.25mi S of junction)

3 1710.9mi, 5:15hr
Access to Mt Ashland Campground (possible water at spring-fed gully)

4 1718.6mi, 8:00hr
Shortcut on L to Callahan's Lodge

5 1719.7mi, 8:30hr
Emerge onto Old Hwy 99 (turn L 0.9mi for Interstate 5 slipway to hitch to Ashland, 0.8mi to Callahan's Lodge), turn R to pass under Interstate 5 onward

SECTION 8 – INTERSTATE 5 (ASHLAND) TO HIGHWAY 242 MCKENZIE PASS

	Stage	Distance (miles)	Total ascent (feet)	Total descent (feet)	Average duration (hr:min)	Page
65	I-5 (Ashland) – Hyatt Lake	23.9	3776	2835	10:00	42
66	Hyatt Lake – Dead Indian Memorial Rd	18.9	2812	2536	8:10	44
67	Dead Indian Memorial Rd – Red Lake Trail	25.2	2667	2047	10:15	47
68	Red Lake Trail – Sevenmile Trail	17.4	1877	2172	7:25	49
69	Sevenmile Trail – Hwy 62	16.8	1969	1604	7:40	51
70	Hwy 62 – Highway 138	26.9	1850	2083	10:00	53
71	Highway 138 – Windigo Pass	30.4	3330	3445	12:30	55
72	Windigo Pass – Hwy 58 Williamette Pass	29.7	3294	4012	12:30	56
73	Hwy 58 Williamette Pass – Irish Lake	22.7	2753	2277	9:30	60
74	Irish Lake – Horse Lake Trail (Elk Lake)	23.2	1486	1755	8:50	63
75	Horse Lake Trail (Elk Lake) – Hwy 242 McKenzie Pass	29.9	3894	3927	12:55	64
Totals		**265**	**29,708**	**28,693**	**109:45**	

WHAT TO EXPECT

As you commence the trail in Oregon, you finally reach the 'flatter, faster' trail that thru-hikers rely on to make up lost time as the seasonal window for thru-hikes begins to shrink. The first 50 miles or so of Oregon are among the lowest trail sections of the whole of Oregon and Washington, and good time can be made. However, it is also one of the driest segments. It is important to hydrate well at water sources before leaving with full bottles. That can mean taking a little more time, but in this way, you can make the most of the limited water that is available.

Initially the land you pass through is criss-crossed with logging roads that can confuse at junctions, so care is required. As you get further into the section you enter Sky Lakes Wilderness, where the number of lakes is greater than any other PCT section. Sadly, the trail visits too few

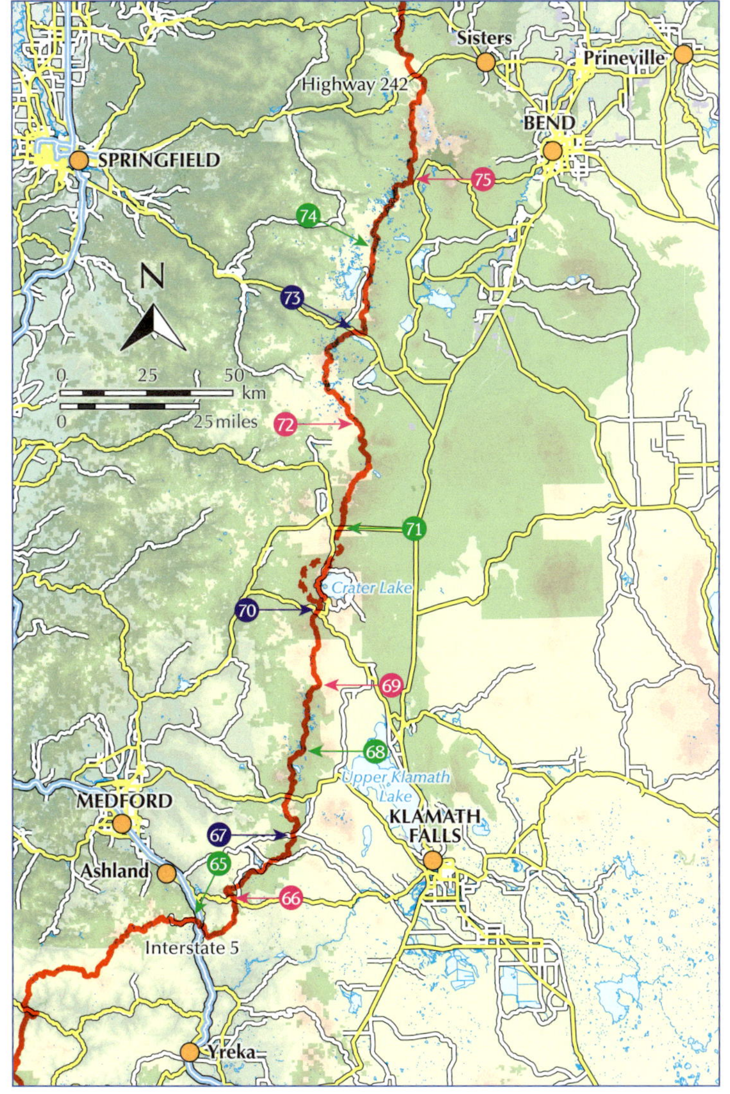
Sisters
Prineville
Highway 242
BEND
SPRINGFIELD
75
74
N
73
0
25
50
km
0
25 miles
72
71
Crater Lake
70
69
68
Upper Klamath Lake
MEDFORD
KLAMATH FALLS
67
65
Ashland
66
Interstate 5
Yreka

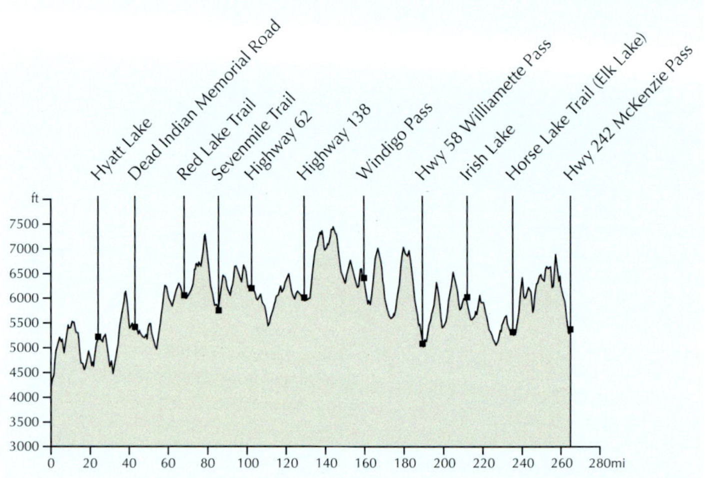

of them. When the route of the old Oregon Skyline Trail (OST) was superseded by the modern PCT route, it was designed to enable equestrian use, and this meant protecting lakes from pollution by equines.

Here you have returned to a landscape dominated by evidence of volcanic activity. None is more obvious than Crater Lake itself, the remnants of Mount Mazama. Of course, this is off the main PCT route which has in practice become the equestrian alternate to the highlight of Crater Lake's Rim Trail. Soon after the two coincide once more and continue north into Mount Thielsen Wilderness, perhaps the most dramatic of Oregon's 'Matterhorns', and the first in a long line of volcanic peaks that steer the hiker toward the dramatic and recent lava field at McKenzie Pass.

In theory the best times to hike are July to late September, when the trail is snow free and before the autumn storms, however finding water could become increasingly challenging beyond late August.

Resupply here is likely to rely on sending packages ahead to one or more of the resorts. Mazama Village is a popular stop, and the facilities and campground are excellent. Shelter Cove too is a common PCT resupply. Both stores have a wide range of snacks and simple resupply items but may not satisfy your requirements for a full resupply.

RESUPPLY OPTIONS

Stage	Trail mile	Place	Off trail (miles)	Description	Facilities
65	1736.5	Green Springs Inn	1.8 SE	Lodging Inn with cabins and restaurant	
65	1743.6	Hyatt Lake Resort	1.4 N	Small resort with cabins, restaurant and limited store	
67	1774.2	Fish Lake Resort	2.0 W	Hiker friendly resort, camping, cabins, accept resupply packages ($)	
70	1822.7	Mazama Village	1.0 SE	Large campground, lodge, restaurant, store accepts packages	
72	1907.6	Shelter Cove	2.2 S	Friendly RV park/resort, camping, store accepts packages ($)	
74	1953.5	Elk Lake Resort	1.4 E	Upmarket resort accepts packages ($), restaurant, camping, small store	
75	1984.7	Sisters	15 E	Mid-size town with good facilities and campground	
75	1984.7	Bend	37 SE	Full service town with hospital and main brand stores	

PERMITS

Permits may be required for overnight trips in Crater Lake National Park, PCT miles 1815.7 to 1848.8.

Permits are required for both day use and overnight stays in Mount Thielsen Wilderness, PCT miles 1859 to 1875.2, and Diamond Peak Wilderness, PCT miles 1891.7 to 1907.2.

Permits are required for overnight trips in Three Sisters Wilderness, PCT miles 1931.6 to 1984.7, Mount Washington Wilderness, PCT miles 1984.7 to 1998.1, and Mount Jefferson Wilderness, PCT miles 2002.4 to 2041.6.

Wizard Island and Crater Lake from the Rim Trail (Stage 70)

Crater Lake National Park

Most hikers who wish to stay overnight in Crater Lake National Park must get a backcountry permit. Permits may be obtained at the backcountry office in park headquarters. PCT thru-hikers alternatively, may sign the trail register as they enter the park: thru-hikers who have signed the trail register do not need to obtain a backcountry permit. Section hikers planning on leaving a vehicle in the park must get a backcountry permit at the ranger station.

For more information call the Crater Lake National Park at (541) 594-3000 or visit: www.nps.gov/crla/planyourvisit/pacific-crest-trail.htm

Mount Thielsen Wilderness

Wilderness Permits are required for both day use and overnight stays from June 15 until October 15. Free, non-quota permits are self-issued at the trailhead.

Diamond Peak Wilderness

Wilderness Permits are required for both day use and overnight stays from Memorial Day Weekend until October 31. Free, non-quota permits are self-issued at the trailhead.

Three Sisters Wilderness/Mount Washington Wilderness/Mount Jefferson Wilderness

Since 2021, special limited-entry permits have been required for hiking in Oregon's Central Cascades Wilderness areas: Three Sisters, Mount Washington and Mount Jefferson.

Permits for the Central Cascades Wilderness areas are available through the recreation.gov website. Approximately 40% of each day's permits are available for advance reservation. The remainder of each day's permits are available seven days in advance of any trip start or area entry.

To obtain a permit visit: www.recreation.gov/permits/4675311

For more information visit: www.pctoregon.com/pct-info/permits

MAIL DROP INFORMATION

Fish Lake Resort
'Your Name Here'
c/o Fish Lake Resort
Hwy 140, Mile Marker 30
Eagle Point, OR 97524
ETA: (Estimated date of arrival)
They are open: Mon–Sun 9am–6pm
Phone them on: (541) 949-8500
Visit them at: www.fishlakeresort.net
(UPS Only)

Crater Lake, Mazama Village
'Your Name', PCT Hiker
c/o Mazama Camper Store
Mazama Village
Crater Lake, OR 97604
ETA: 'Your ETA'
They are open: Mon–Sun 8am–8pm
Phone them on: (866) 292-6720
Visit them at: www.nps.gov/crla/planyourvisit/pacific-crest-trail.htm

Shelter Cove Resort
27600 West Odell Lake Road, Hwy 58
Crescent Lake, OR 97733
Please Hold for 'Your Name'
Phone them on: (541) 433-2548
Visit them at: www.sheltercoveresort.com

Elk Lake Resort
6000 Century Drive
Bend, OR 97701
Please Hold for 'Your Name'
Estimated Date of Arrival: 'Your ETA'
They are open: Mon–Sun 9am–6pm
Phone them on: (541) 480-7378
Visit them at: www.elklakeresort.net
(UPS/FedEx Only)

POST OFFICE INFORMATION

'Your Name Here'
c/o General Delivery
Sisters, OR 97759
Located at: 694 N Larch Street
Phone them on: (541) 549-0412

'Your Name Here'
c\o General Delivery
Bend, OR 97703
Located at: 61 NW Oregon Avenue
Phone them on: (541) 318-5068

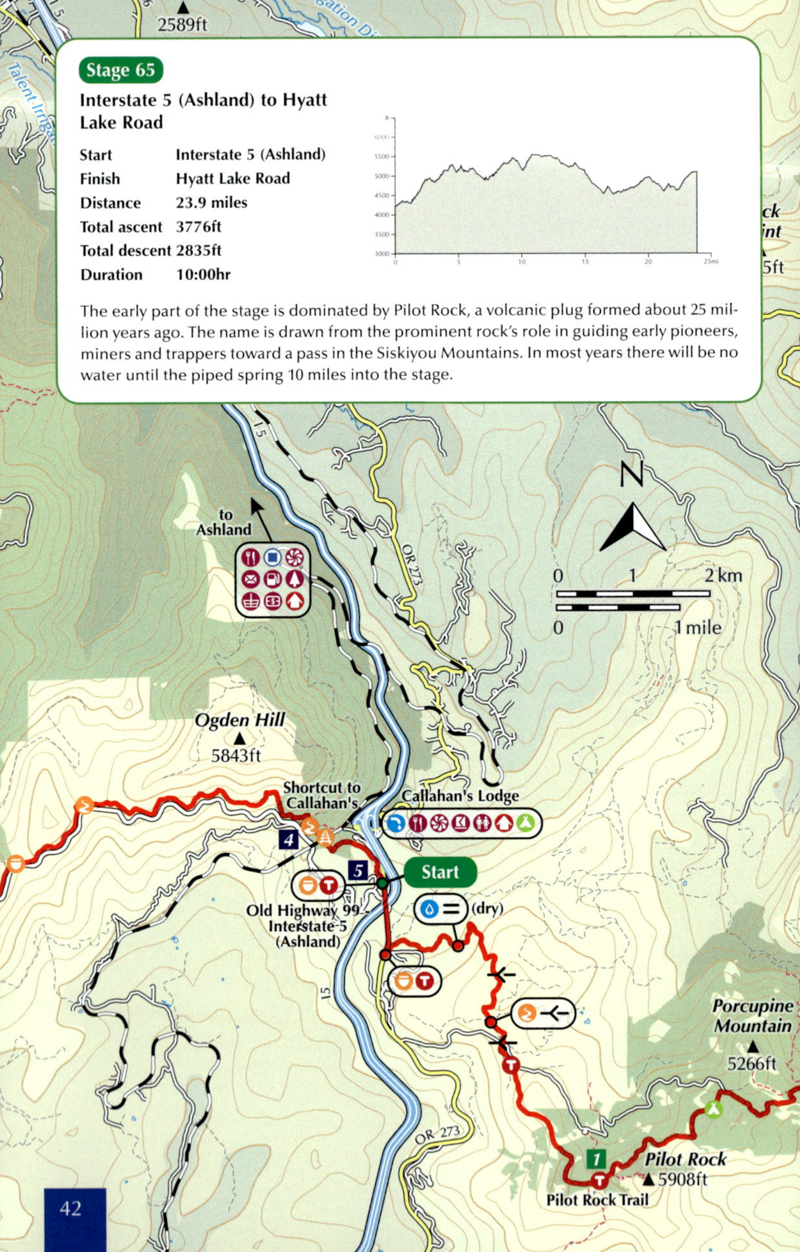

Butte
2589ft
Stage 65
Interstate 5 (Ashland) to Hyatt Lake Road
Start Interstate 5 (Ashland)
Finish Hyatt Lake Road
Distance 23.9 miles
Total ascent 3776ft
Total descent 2835ft
Duration 10:00hr
The early part of the stage is dominated by Pilot Rock, a volcanic plug formed about 25 million years ago. The name is drawn from the prominent rock's role in guiding early pioneers, miners and trappers toward a pass in the Siskiyou Mountains. In most years there will be no water until the piped spring 10 miles into the stage.
to Ashland
N
0 1 2 km
0 1 mile
OR 273
Ogden Hill
5843ft
Shortcut to Callahan's
Callahan's Lodge
4
5
Start
(dry)
Old Highway 99 – Interstate 5 (Ashland)
15
OR 273
Porcupine Mountain
5266ft
1
Pilot Rock
5908ft
Pilot Rock Trail

Stage 65 route waypoints

From the Old Hwy 99/Interstate 5 trailhead, walk 0.5mi S passing under Interstate 5 then take signed PCT trail L off highway

1 **1724.5mi, 1:55hr**
Having crossed two dirt roads, keep L past Pilot Rock Trail

2 **1729.1mi, 4:20hr**
Just beyond Lone Pilot Trail junction find Piped Spring and campgrounds

3 **1736.5mi, 7:20hr**
Cross Hwy 66 at Green Springs Summit (Green Springs Inn 1.8mi SE)

4 **1742.1mi, 9:15hr**
Little Hyatt Reservoir outlet

5 **1743.6mi, 10:00hr**
Cross Hyatt Lake Road, Hyatt Lake Resort 1.4mi N, very small store

Keep an eye open for the peregrine falcons that regularly nest on Pilot Rock. For this reason, the rock is closed to climbers until end July.

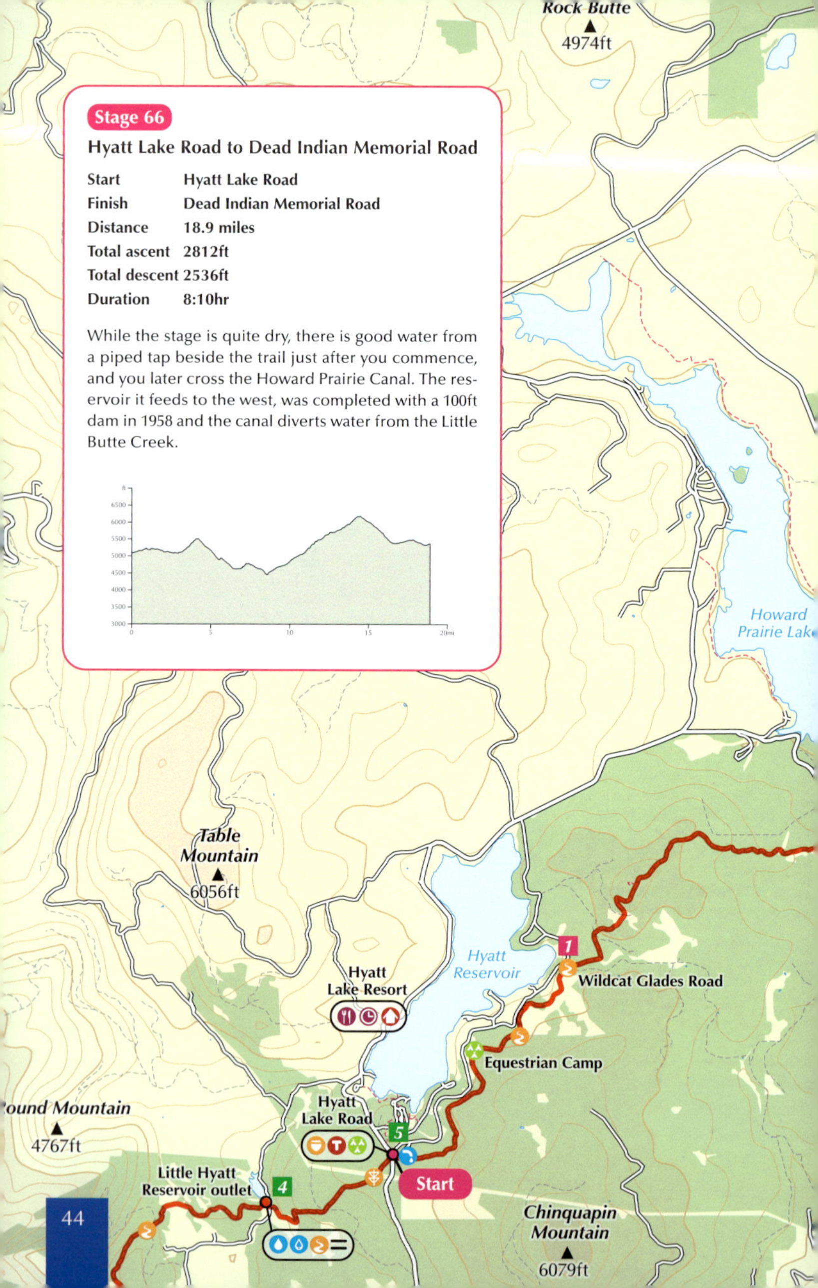
Stage 66
Hyatt Lake Road to Dead Indian Memorial Road
Start Hyatt Lake Road
Finish Dead Indian Memorial Road
Distance 18.9 miles
Total ascent 2812ft
Total descent 2536ft
Duration 8:10hr
While the stage is quite dry, there is good water from a piped tap beside the trail just after you commence, and you later cross the Howard Prairie Canal. The reservoir it feeds to the west, was completed with a 100ft dam in 1958 and the canal diverts water from the Little Butte Creek.
Rock Butte
4974ft
Howard Prairie Lak
Table Mountain
6056ft
Hyatt Reservoir
Hyatt Lake Resort
Wildcat Glades Road
Equestrian Camp
ound Mountain
4767ft
Hyatt Lake Road
Start
Little Hyatt Reservoir outlet
Chinquapin Mountain
6079ft
1
4
5

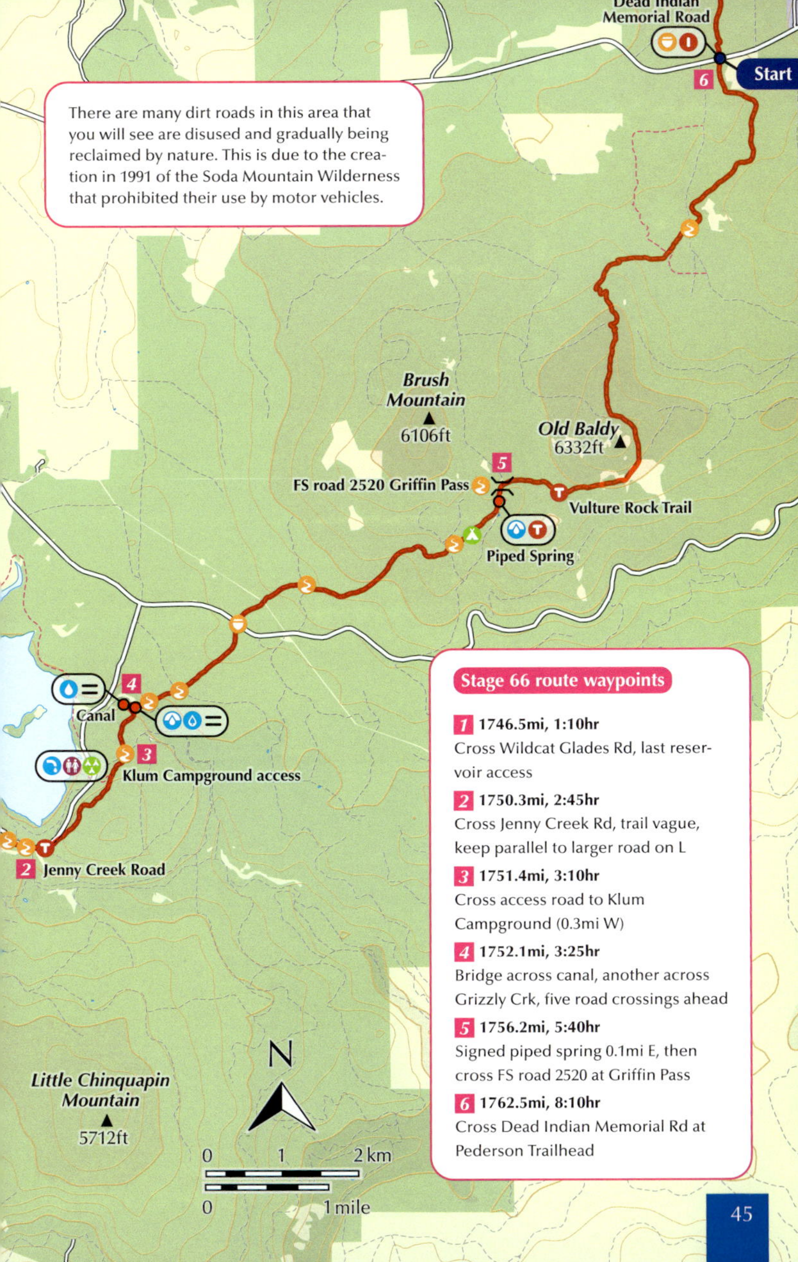

Dead Indian Memorial Road
Start
6
There are many dirt roads in this area that you will see are disused and gradually being reclaimed by nature. This is due to the creation in 1991 of the Soda Mountain Wilderness that prohibited their use by motor vehicles.
Brush Mountain
6106ft
Old Baldy
6332ft
5
FS road 2520 Griffin Pass
Vulture Rock Trail
Piped Spring
4
Canal
3
Klum Campground access
2
Jenny Creek Road
Little Chinquapin Mountain
5712ft
N
0
1
2 km
0
1 mile
Stage 66 route waypoints
1 1746.5mi, 1:10hr
Cross Wildcat Glades Rd, last reservoir access
2 1750.3mi, 2:45hr
Cross Jenny Creek Rd, trail vague, keep parallel to larger road on L
3 1751.4mi, 3:10hr
Cross access road to Klum Campground (0.3mi W)
4 1752.1mi, 3:25hr
Bridge across canal, another across Grizzly Crk, five road crossings ahead
5 1756.2mi, 5:40hr
Signed piped spring 0.1mi E, then cross FS road 2520 at Griffin Pass
6 1762.5mi, 8:10hr
Cross Dead Indian Memorial Rd at Pederson Trailhead

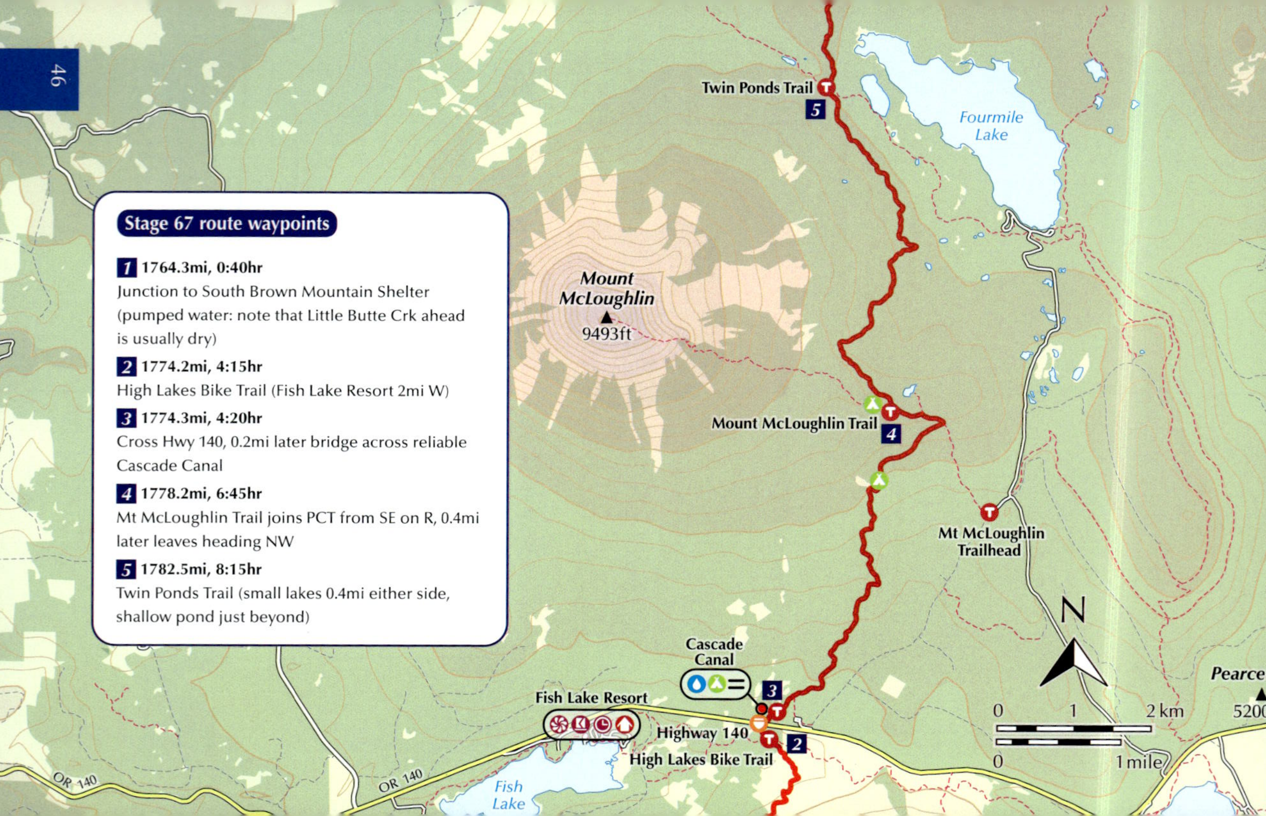

Stage 67 route waypoints

1 **1764.3mi, 0:40hr**
Junction to South Brown Mountain Shelter (pumped water: note that Little Butte Crk ahead is usually dry)

2 **1774.2mi, 4:15hr**
High Lakes Bike Trail (Fish Lake Resort 2mi W)

3 **1774.3mi, 4:20hr**
Cross Hwy 140, 0.2mi later bridge across reliable Cascade Canal

4 **1778.2mi, 6:45hr**
Mt McLoughlin Trail joins PCT from SE on R, 0.4mi later leaves heading NW

5 **1782.5mi, 8:15hr**
Twin Ponds Trail (small lakes 0.4mi either side, shallow pond just beyond)

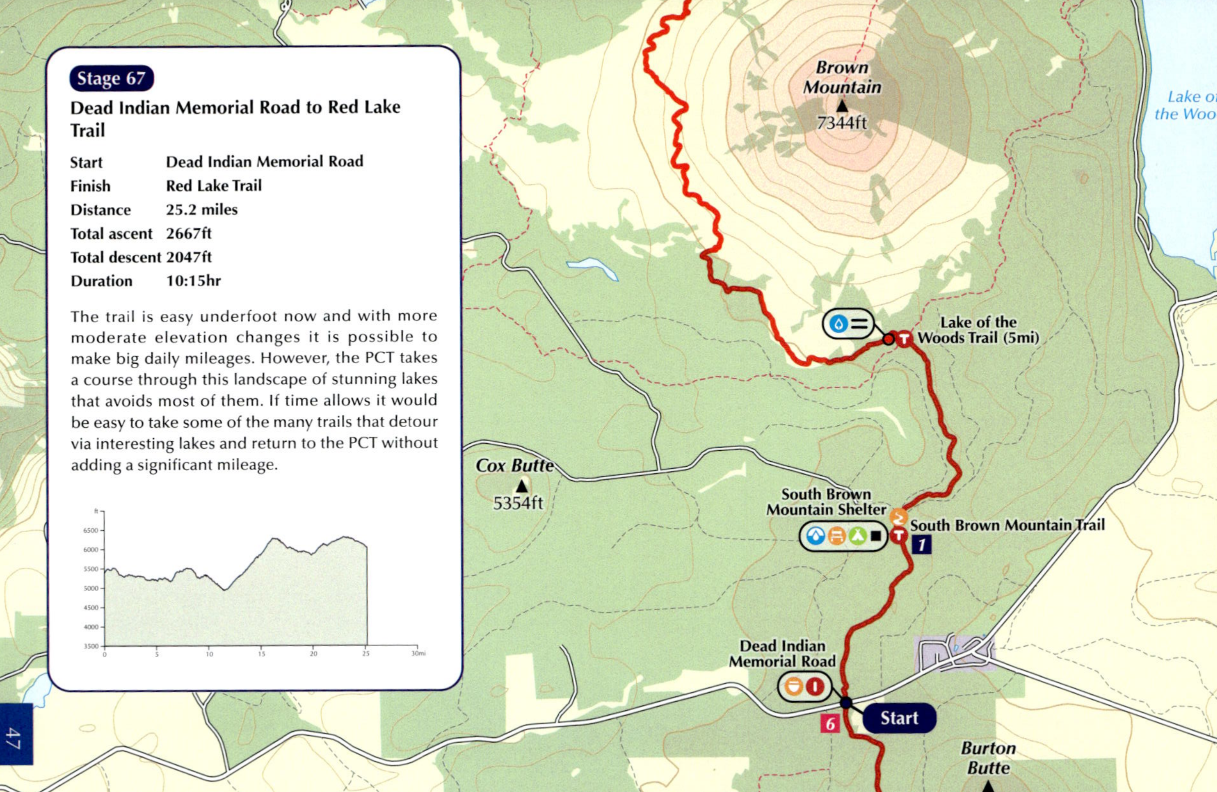

Stage 67

Dead Indian Memorial Road to Red Lake Trail

Start	**Dead Indian Memorial Road**
Finish	**Red Lake Trail**
Distance	**25.2 miles**
Total ascent	**2667ft**
Total descent	**2047ft**
Duration	**10:15hr**

The trail is easy underfoot now and with more moderate elevation changes it is possible to make big daily mileages. However, the PCT takes a course through this landscape of stunning lakes that avoids most of them. If time allows it would be easy to take some of the many trails that detour via interesting lakes and return to the PCT without adding a significant mileage.

Stage 68 route waypoints

1 **1790.4mi, 0:55hr**
Red Lake Trail rejoins from W

2 **1791.3mi, 1:15hr**
Keep L as Sky Lakes Trail departs NE (becoming Snow Lakes Trail)

3 **1796.9mi, 3:50hr**
Snow Lakes Trail connects to PCT from NE

4 **1798.7mi, 4:55hr**
Keep R at fork with Devil's Peak Trail (to Seven Lakes Trail)

5 **1801.8mi, 6:05hr**
Keep R as Seven Lakes Trail (first) connects from SW

6 **1802.0mi, 6:10hr**
Creek above Grass Lake (likely last water before Mazama Village)

7 **1802.5mi, 6:25hr**
Keep R as Seven Lakes Trail (second) connects from W

8 **1805.1mi, 7:25hr**
Sevenmile Trail junction (1.8mi NE to trailhead)

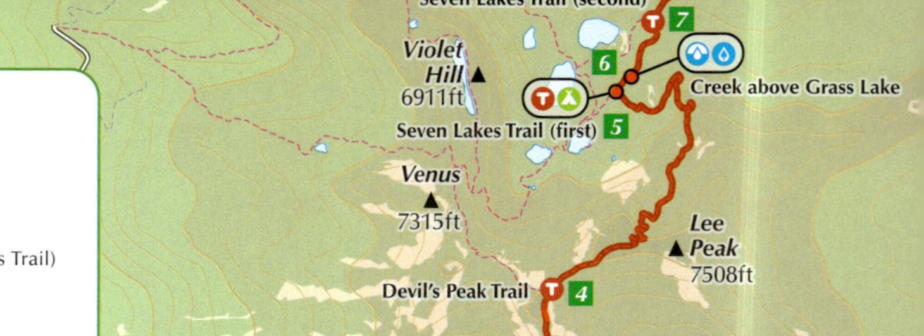

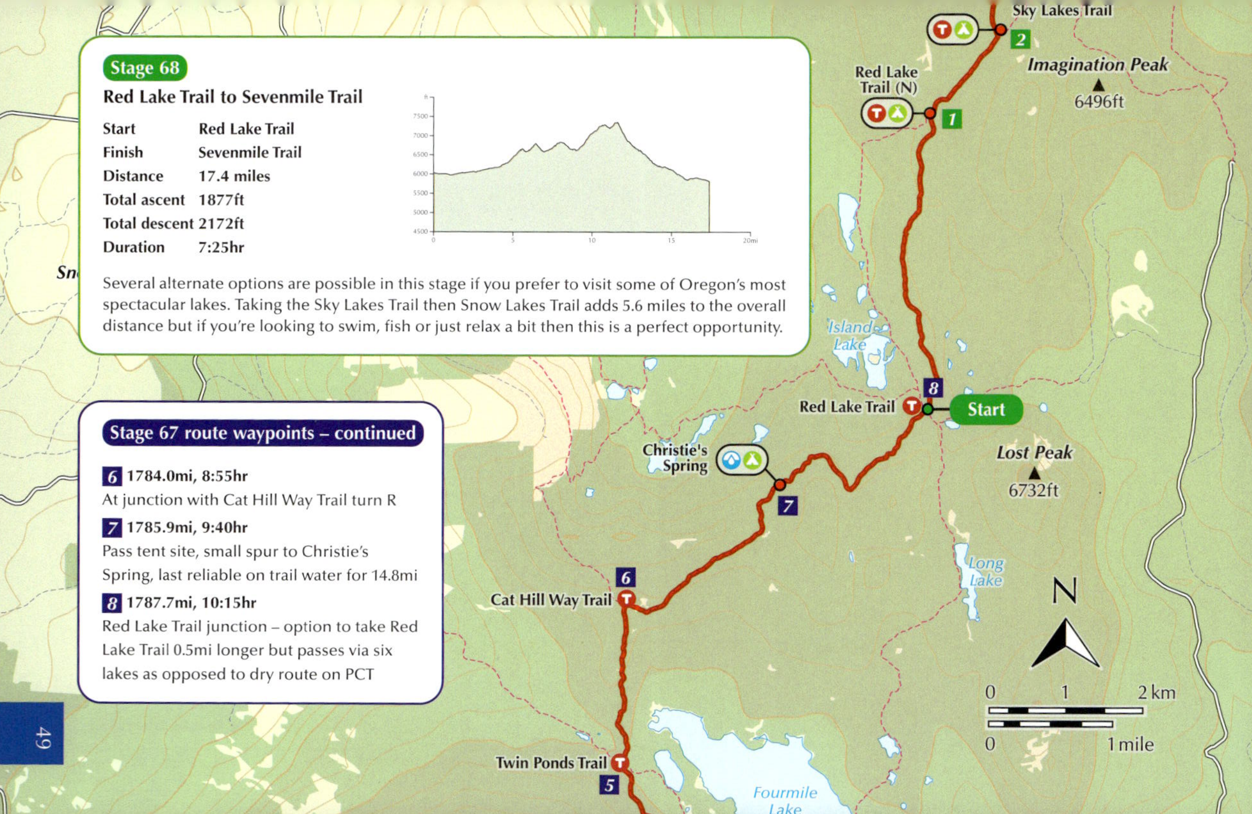

Stage 68

Red Lake Trail to Sevenmile Trail

Start	Red Lake Trail
Finish	Sevenmile Trail
Distance	17.4 miles
Total ascent	1877ft
Total descent	2172ft
Duration	7:25hr

Several alternate options are possible in this stage if you prefer to visit some of Oregon's most spectacular lakes. Taking the Sky Lakes Trail then Snow Lakes Trail adds 5.6 miles to the overall distance but if you're looking to swim, fish or just relax a bit then this is a perfect opportunity.

Stage 67 route waypoints – continued

6 1784.0mi, 8:55hr
At junction with Cat Hill Way Trail turn R

7 1785.9mi, 9:40hr
Pass tent site, small spur to Christie's Spring, last reliable on trail water for 14.8mi

8 1787.7mi, 10:15hr
Red Lake Trail junction – option to take Red Lake Trail 0.5mi longer but passes via six lakes as opposed to dry route on PCT

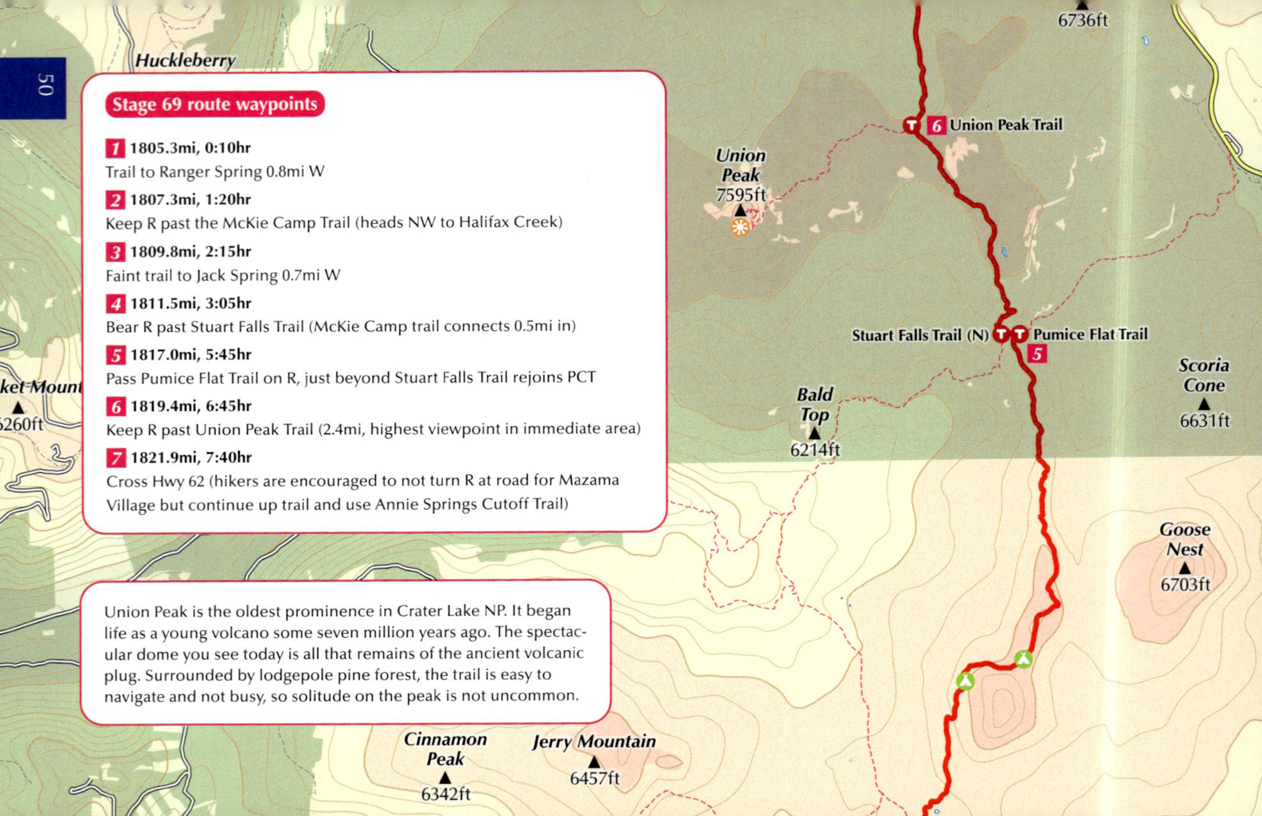

Stage 69 route waypoints

1 1805.3mi, 0:10hr
Trail to Ranger Spring 0.8mi W

2 1807.3mi, 1:20hr
Keep R past the McKie Camp Trail (heads NW to Halifax Creek)

3 1809.8mi, 2:15hr
Faint trail to Jack Spring 0.7mi W

4 1811.5mi, 3:05hr
Bear R past Stuart Falls Trail (McKie Camp trail connects 0.5mi in)

5 1817.0mi, 5:45hr
Pass Pumice Flat Trail on R, just beyond Stuart Falls Trail rejoins PCT

6 1819.4mi, 6:45hr
Keep R past Union Peak Trail (2.4mi, highest viewpoint in immediate area)

7 1821.9mi, 7:40hr
Cross Hwy 62 (hikers are encouraged to not turn R at road for Mazama Village but continue up trail and use Annie Springs Cutoff Trail)

Union Peak is the oldest prominence in Crater Lake NP. It began life as a young volcano some seven million years ago. The spectacular dome you see today is all that remains of the ancient volcanic plug. Surrounded by lodgepole pine forest, the trail is easy to navigate and not busy, so solitude on the peak is not uncommon.

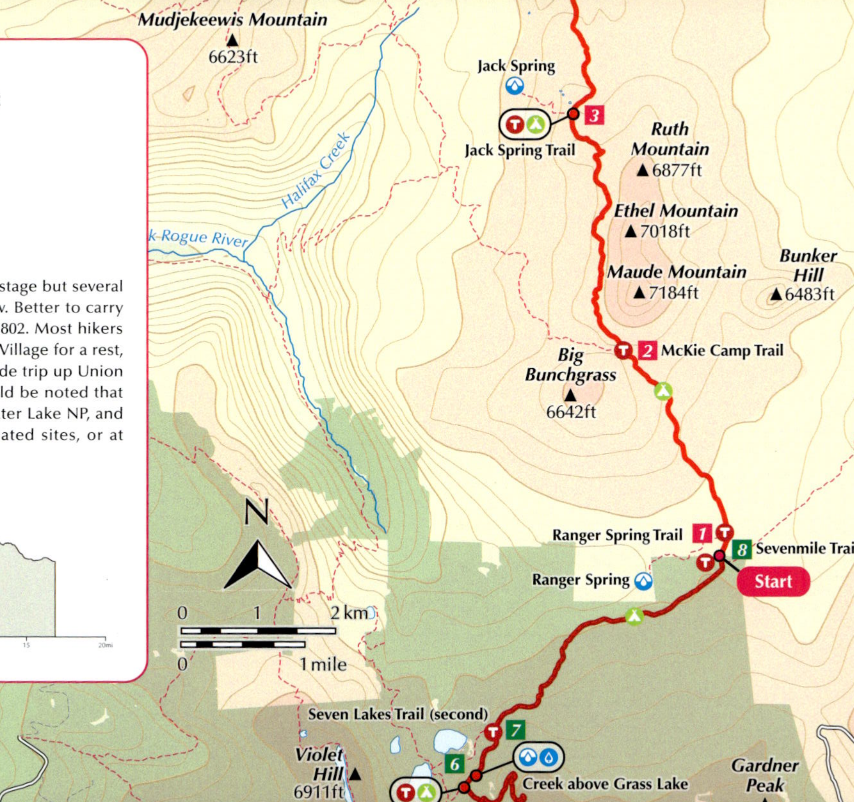

Stage 69

Sevenmile Trail to Highway 62

Start	Sevenmile Trail
Finish	Highway 62
Distance	16.8 miles
Total ascent	1969ft
Total descent	1604ft
Duration	7:40hr

There is no water on trail in this stage but several options off trail are noted below. Better to carry enough from the creek at mile 1802. Most hikers will be keen to get into Mazama Village for a rest, but if you can make the time a side trip up Union Peak is worth the effort. It should be noted that hitch-hiking is prohibited in Crater Lake NP, and camping is restricted to designated sites, or at least one mile from any road.

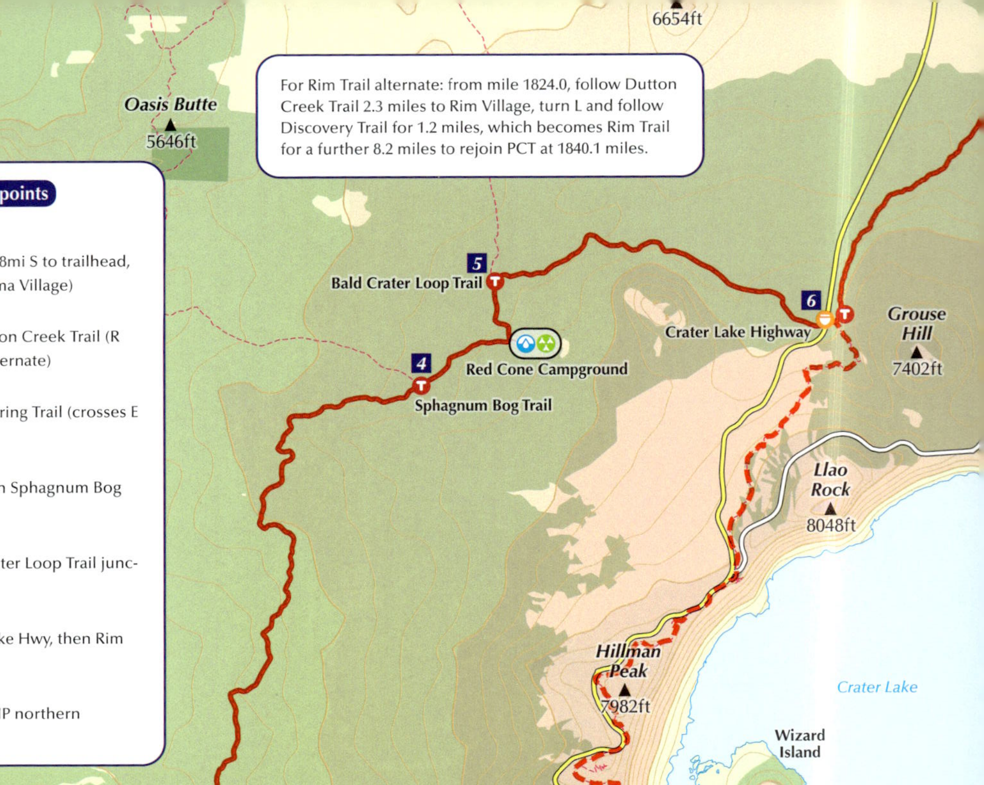

For Rim Trail alternate: from mile 1824.0, follow Dutton Creek Trail 2.3 miles to Rim Village, turn L and follow Discovery Trail for 1.2 miles, which becomes Rim Trail for a further 8.2 miles to rejoin PCT at 1840.1 miles.

Stage 70 route waypoints

1 1822.7mi, 0:30hr
Annie Springs Trail, (0.8mi S to trailhead, 0.2mi further to Mazama Village)

2 1824.0mi, 1:00hr
Keep L for PCT at Dutton Creek Trail (R for Crater Lake Rim alternate)

3 1828.4mi, 2:35hr
Keep L at Lightning Spring Trail (crosses E to join Rim Trail)

4 1835.3mi, 5:15hr
Keep R at junction with Sphagnum Bog Trail

5 1836.9mi, 5:45hr
Take R fork at Bald Crater Loop Trail junction to stay on PCT

6 1840.1mi, 6:55hr
Cross paved Crater Lake Hwy, then Rim Trail rejoins from SE

7 1848.8mi, 10:00hr
Hwy 138 Crater Lake NP northern boundary

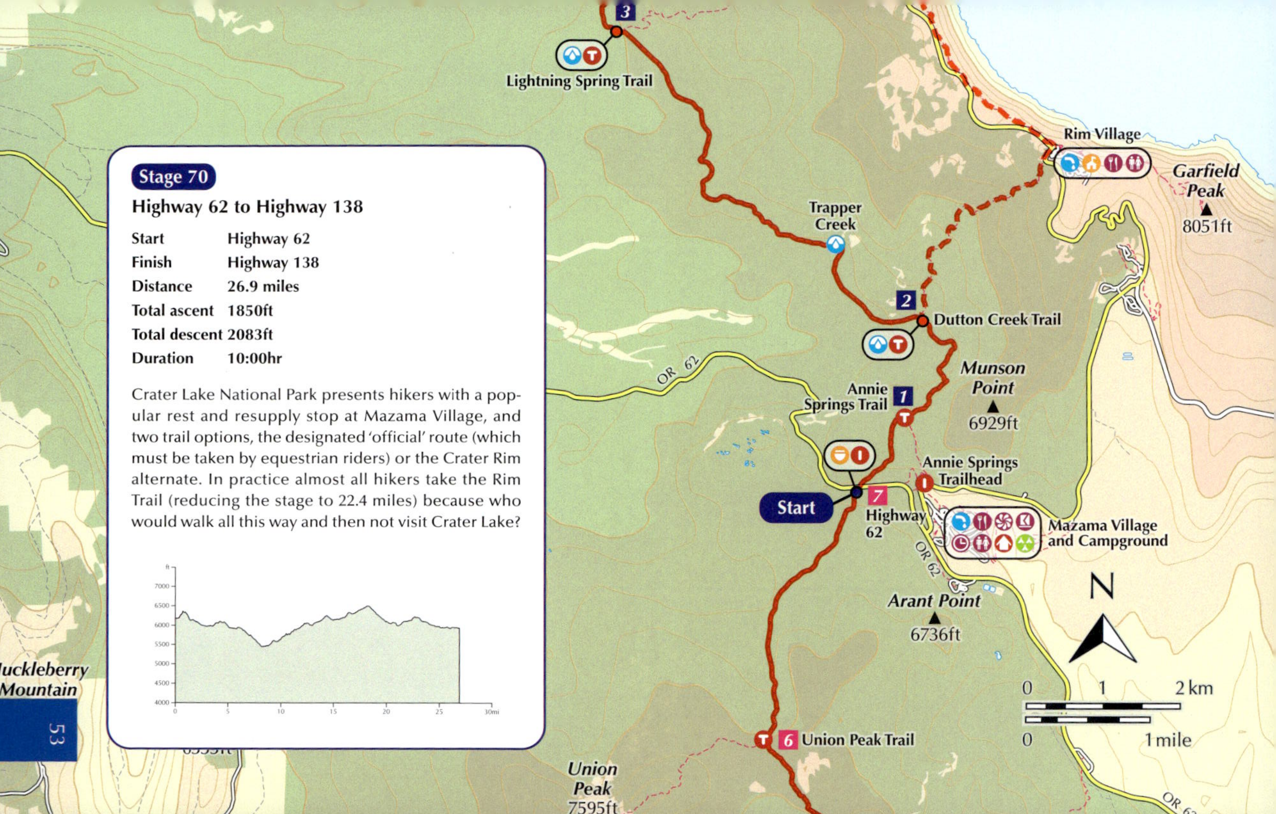

Stage 70

Highway 62 to Highway 138

Start	**Highway 62**
Finish	**Highway 138**
Distance	**26.9 miles**
Total ascent	**1850ft**
Total descent	**2083ft**
Duration	**10:00hr**

Crater Lake National Park presents hikers with a popular rest and resupply stop at Mazama Village, and two trail options, the designated 'official' route (which must be taken by equestrian riders) or the Crater Rim alternate. In practice almost all hikers take the Rim Trail (reducing the stage to 22.4 miles) because who would walk all this way and then not visit Crater Lake?

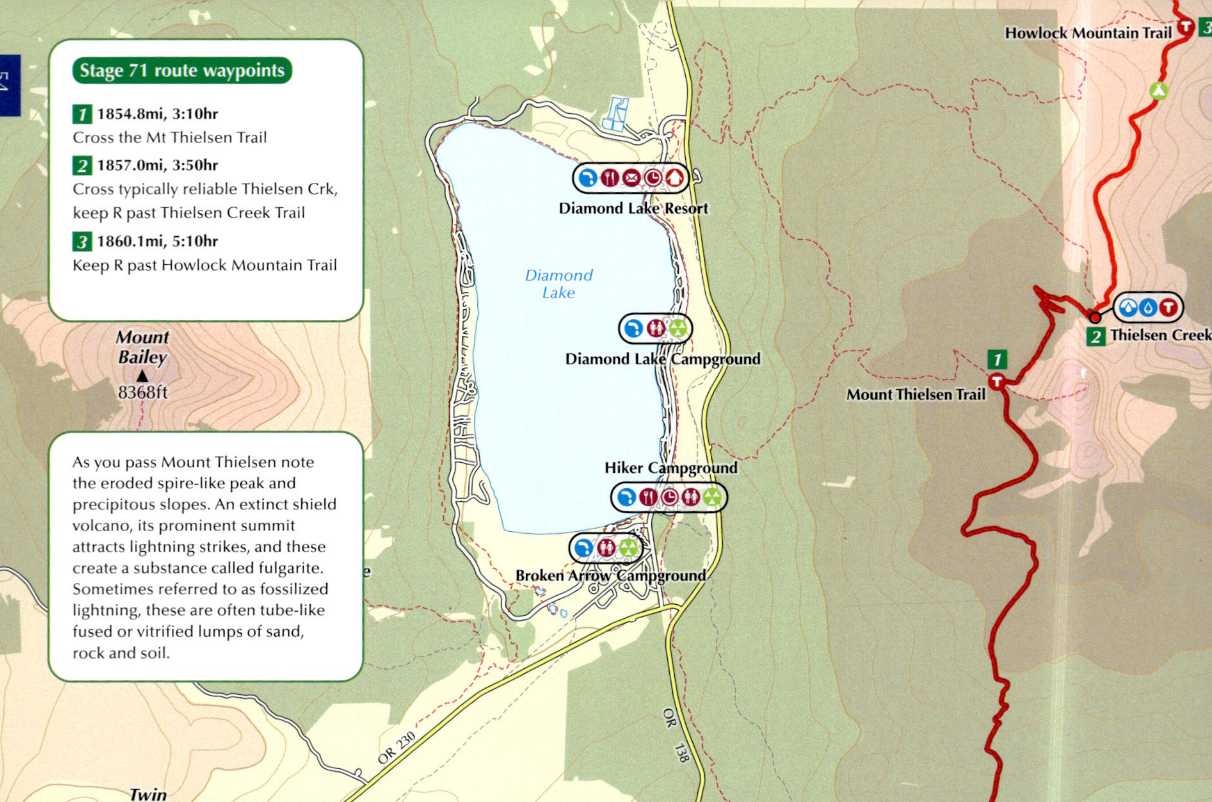

Stage 71 route waypoints

1 **1854.8mi, 3:10hr**
Cross the Mt Thielsen Trail

2 **1857.0mi, 3:50hr**
Cross typically reliable Thielsen Crk, keep R past Thielsen Creek Trail

3 **1860.1mi, 5:10hr**
Keep R past Howlock Mountain Trail

As you pass Mount Thielsen note the eroded spire-like peak and precipitous slopes. An extinct shield volcano, its prominent summit attracts lightning strikes, and these create a substance called fulgarite. Sometimes referred to as fossilized lightning, these are often tube-like fused or vitrified lumps of sand, rock and soil.

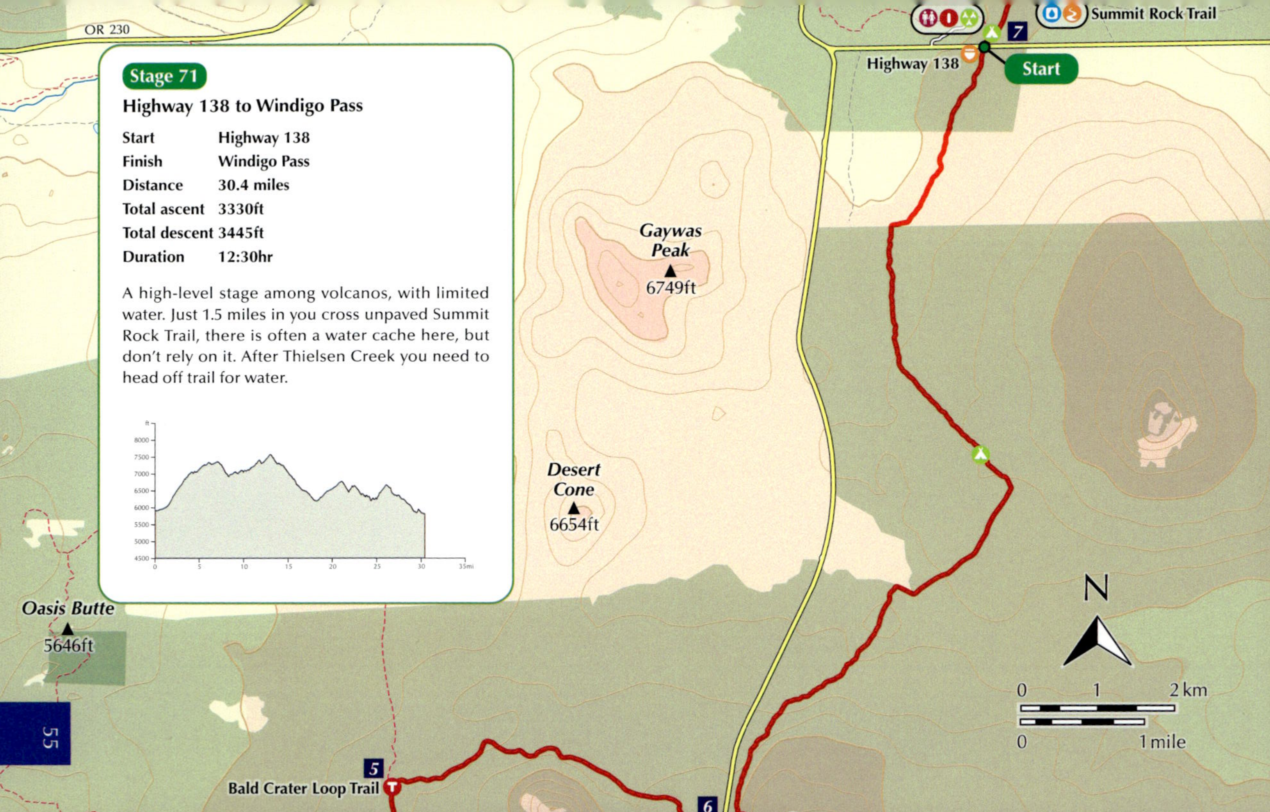

Stage 71

Highway 138 to Windigo Pass

Start	Highway 138
Finish	Windigo Pass
Distance	30.4 miles
Total ascent	3330ft
Total descent	3445ft
Duration	12:30hr

A high-level stage among volcanos, with limited water. Just 1.5 miles in you cross unpaved Summit Rock Trail, there is often a water cache here, but don't rely on it. After Thielsen Creek you need to head off trail for water.

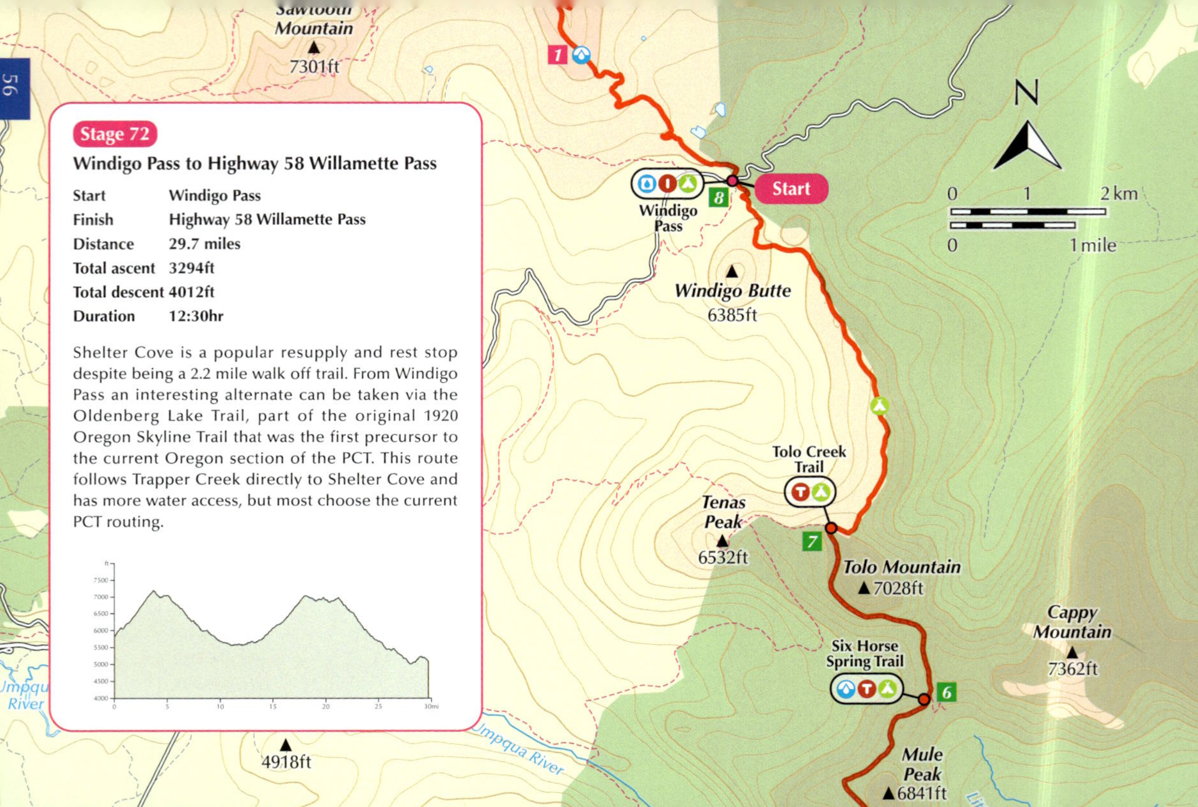

Stage 72

Windigo Pass to Highway 58 Willamette Pass

Start	Windigo Pass
Finish	Highway 58 Willamette Pass
Distance	29.7 miles
Total ascent	3294ft
Total descent	4012ft
Duration	12:30hr

Shelter Cove is a popular resupply and rest stop despite being a 2.2 mile walk off trail. From Windigo Pass an interesting alternate can be taken via the Oldenberg Lake Trail, part of the original 1920 Oregon Skyline Trail that was the first precursor to the current Oregon section of the PCT. This route follows Trapper Creek directly to Shelter Cove and has more water access, but most choose the current PCT routing.

Stage 71 route waypoints – continued
4 1861.7mi, 5:50hr
Oregon and Washington PCT high point: (sign states 7560ft, actually 7572ft)
5 1866.9mi, 7:40hr
North Umpqua Trail to Maidu Lake (0.75mi NW)
6 1873.1mi, 9:45hr
Six Horse Spring Trail (spring 0.4mi E, 300ft descent)
7 1875.1mi, 10:45hr
Keep R past Tolo Creek Trail
8 1879.2mi, 12:30hr
Cross dirt road at Windigo Pass
Red Cinder Butte
6545ft
Miller Mountain
7503ft
Maidu Lake
North Umpqua Trail
5
Wits End
6604ft
Tipsoo Peak
8005ft
Red Cone
7254ft
4
OR/WA PCT high point
OR 138
Howlock Mountain Trail
3
Howlock Mountain
8396ft

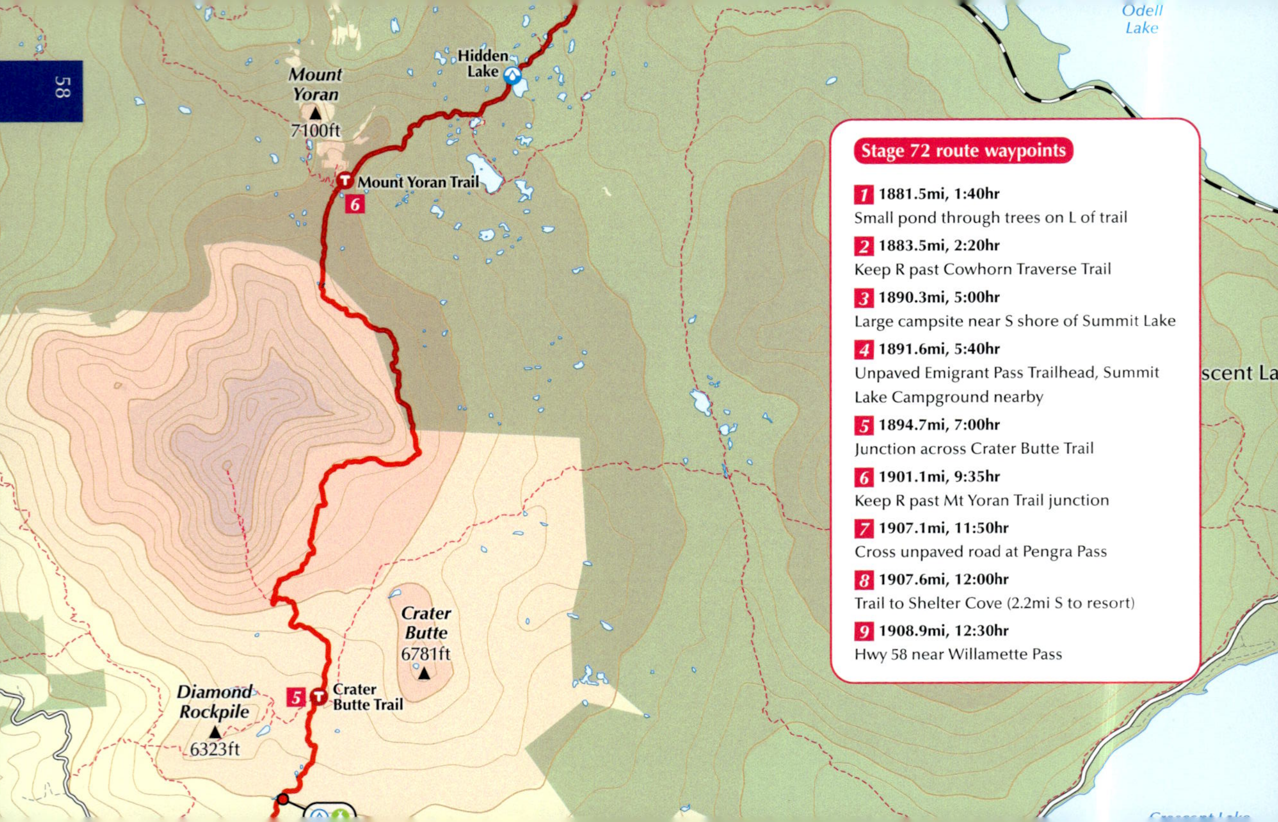

Stage 72 route waypoints

1 1881.5mi, 1:40hr
Small pond through trees on L of trail

2 1883.5mi, 2:20hr
Keep R past Cowhorn Traverse Trail

3 1890.3mi, 5:00hr
Large campsite near S shore of Summit Lake

4 1891.6mi, 5:40hr
Unpaved Emigrant Pass Trailhead, Summit Lake Campground nearby

5 1894.7mi, 7:00hr
Junction across Crater Butte Trail

6 1901.1mi, 9:35hr
Keep R past Mt Yoran Trail junction

7 1907.1mi, 11:50hr
Cross unpaved road at Pengra Pass

8 1907.6mi, 12:00hr
Trail to Shelter Cove (2.2mi S to resort)

9 1908.9mi, 12:30hr
Hwy 58 near Willamette Pass

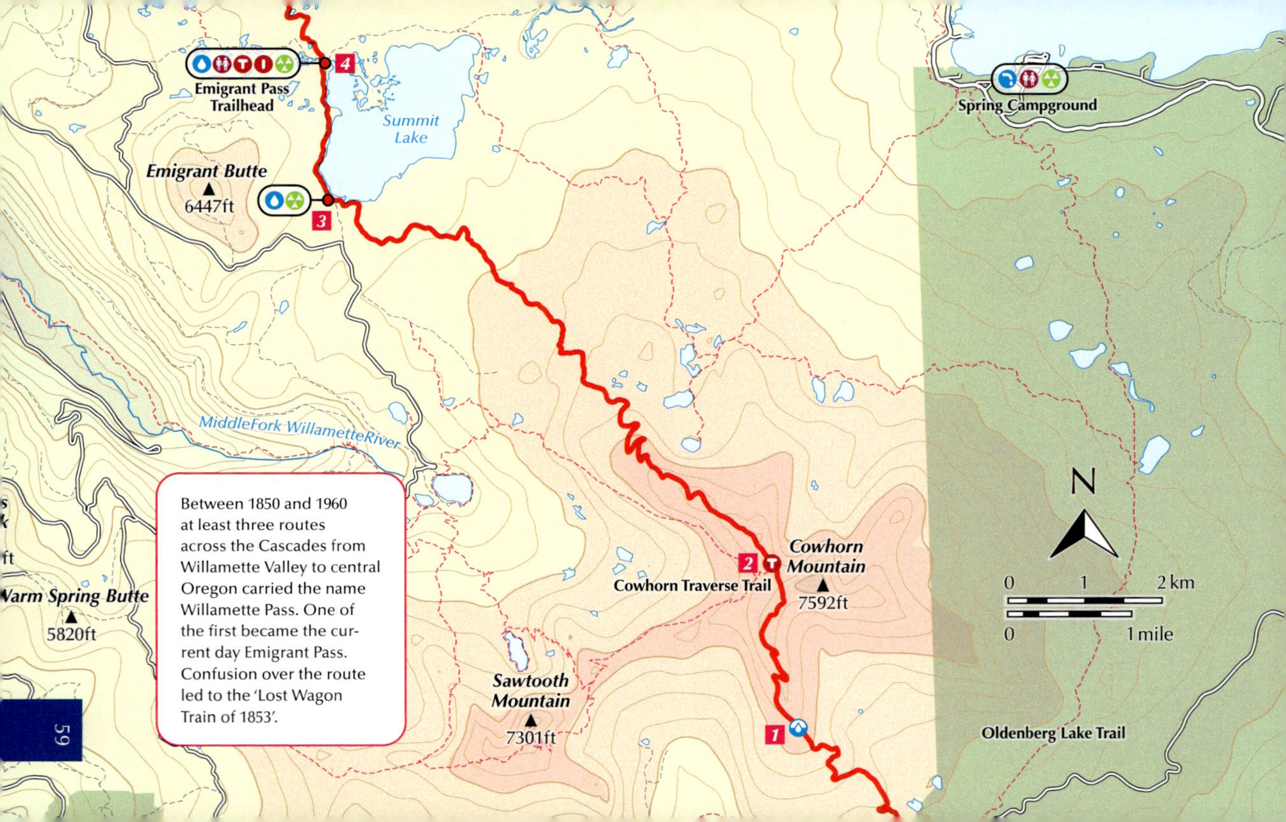

Between 1850 and 1960 at least three routes across the Cascades from Willamette Valley to central Oregon carried the name Willamette Pass. One of the first became the current day Emigrant Pass. Confusion over the route led to the 'Lost Wagon Train of 1853'.

Stage 73

Highway 58 Willamette Pass to Irish Lake

Start	**Highway 58 Willamette Pass**
Finish	**Irish Lake**
Distance	**22.7 miles**
Total ascent	**2753ft**
Total descent	**2277ft**
Duration	**9:30hr**

An undulating and largely forested stage with good trail makes for easy going. Fans of English football (soccer in the US) may notice that they pass both Bobby Lake (accessed by Moore Creek Trail) and Charlton Lake in close succession in this stage. Despite the coincidence, there is no connection to either of the late, great footballers that I can find.

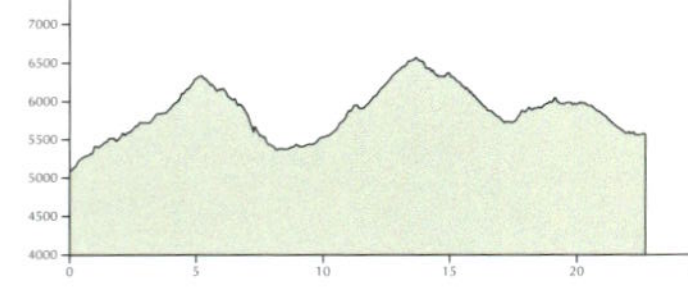

Stage 73 route waypoints

1 **1911.8mi, 1:20hr**
Meet Lower Rosary Lake, continue NE along shore

2 **1913.1mi, 2:10hr**
Keep L at fork for Maiden Peak Trail (S), climb to saddle then keep R, NE

3 **1916.2mi, 3:15hr**
Cross ahead at junction with Maiden Peak Trail (N)

4 **1918.6mi, 4:05hr**
Cross Bobby Lake/Moore Creek Trails junction (Bobby Lake 0.3mi E)

5 **1926.1mi, 7:20hr**
Cross Charlton Lake Trail with lake access and camping

6 **1926.6mi, 7:35hr**
Keep ahead across FS dirt road 4290

7 **1931.6mi, 9:30hr**
Cross unpaved FS road 600 between Taylor Lake and Irish Lake

FS road 4290
Charlton Lake Trail
Charlton Lake
Gerdine Butte
6493ft
The Twins
7362ft
Twin Peaks Trail
Bobby Lake/Moore Creek Trails
Bobby Lake
Mount Ray
7001ft
Fuji Mountain
7142ft
t David

In 1927, the railroad opened taking the Pengra Pass route. Subsequently the road became established at its current location, becoming Highway 58 in 1932, with definitive naming of the routes confirmed in 1960 by the Oregon Geographic Names Board.
Maiden Peak Trail (N)
3
Maiden Peak Shelter
Maiden Peak
7823ft
Gold Lake
Salt Creek
OR 58
OR 58
OR 58
OR 58
Maiden Peak Trail (S)
2
Lower Rosary Lake
1
Start
9
Shelter Cove Trail
8
Pengra Pass
7
Willamette Pass
Shelter Cove Resort
Odell Lake
N
0
1
2 km
0
1 mile
Hidden Lake
Mount Yoran
7100ft
Mount Yoran Trail
6

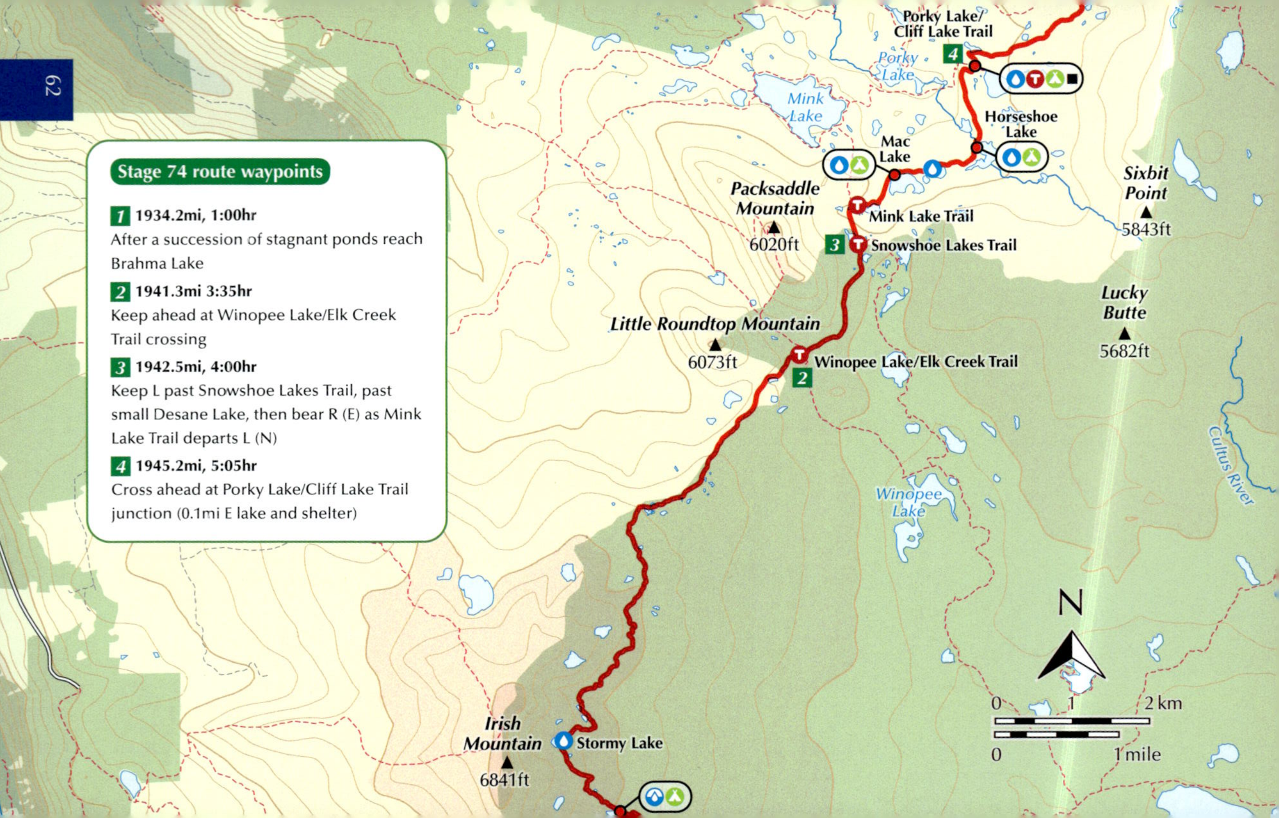

Stage 74 route waypoints

1 **1934.2mi, 1:00hr**
After a succession of stagnant ponds reach Brahma Lake

2 **1941.3mi 3:35hr**
Keep ahead at Winopee Lake/Elk Creek Trail crossing

3 **1942.5mi, 4:00hr**
Keep L past Snowshoe Lakes Trail, past small Desane Lake, then bear R (E) as Mink Lake Trail departs L (N)

4 **1945.2mi, 5:05hr**
Cross ahead at Porky Lake/Cliff Lake Trail junction (0.1mi E lake and shelter)

Stage 74

Irish Lake to Horse Lake Trail (Elk Lake)

Start	**Irish Lake**
Finish	**Horse Lake Trail (Elk Lake)**
Distance	**23.2 miles**
Total ascent	**1486ft**
Total descent	**1755ft**
Duration	**8:50hr**

Well signposted trail junctions through much of Oregon makes route finding easier. Elk Lake Resort is a rustic, lakeside campsite with cabins and limited facilities but very friendly toward hikers. Most will use this as an overnight stop with dinner and breakfast rather than a resupply.

Beyond Charlton Lake you hike through an area struggling to recover from a large fire in 2000. As in similar areas, what is left behind after a fire are 'ghost trees', the blackened trunks that remain standing. Treat these with caution, they will eventually fall. Never camp below or among dead trees. Always look up as well as around for hazards when you are choosing a pitch.

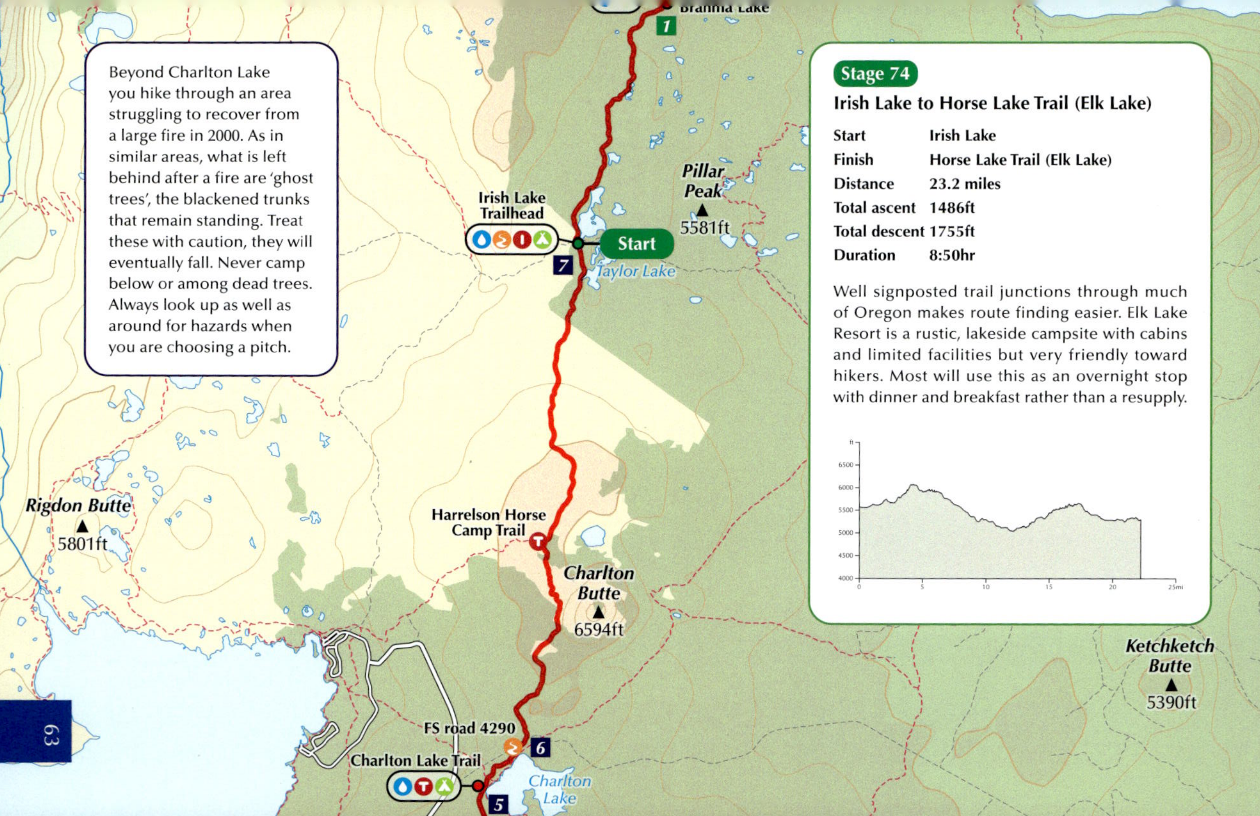

Stage 75

Horse Lake Trail (Elk Lake) to Highway 242 McKenzie Pass

Start	Horse Lake Trail (Elk Lake)
Finish	Highway 242 McKenzie Pass
Distance	29.9 miles
Total ascent	3894ft
Total descent	3927ft
Duration	12:55hr

This stage is dominated by views of the Three Sisters volcanos as you traverse their western slopes. Where previously you have trodden across ancient volcanic deposits, here you will at times walk across solidified lava flows as recent as 200 years old. Note that the coarse rock can destroy trail shoes. Few hikers want to replace their footwear until north of Santiam Pass.

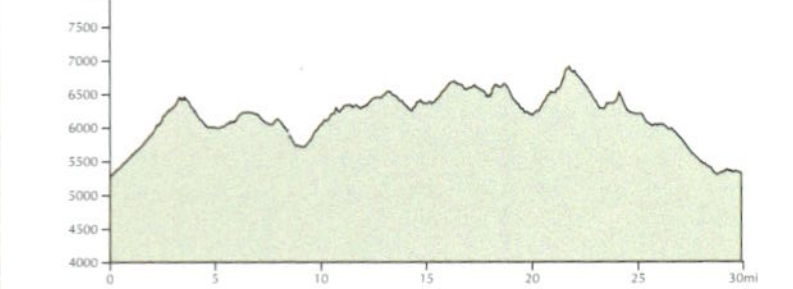

Stage 75 route waypoints

1 **1959.5mi, 2:15hr**
Pass Red Hill Trail, Sisters Mirror Lake, across Nash Lake/Mirror Lakes Trail

2 **1963.0mi, 3:55hr**
North Fork Mesa Creek (sensitive meadow area – no camping nearby)

3 **1968.9mi, 6:10hr**
Keep R past Foley Ridge Trail and subsequent Linton Meadow Trail

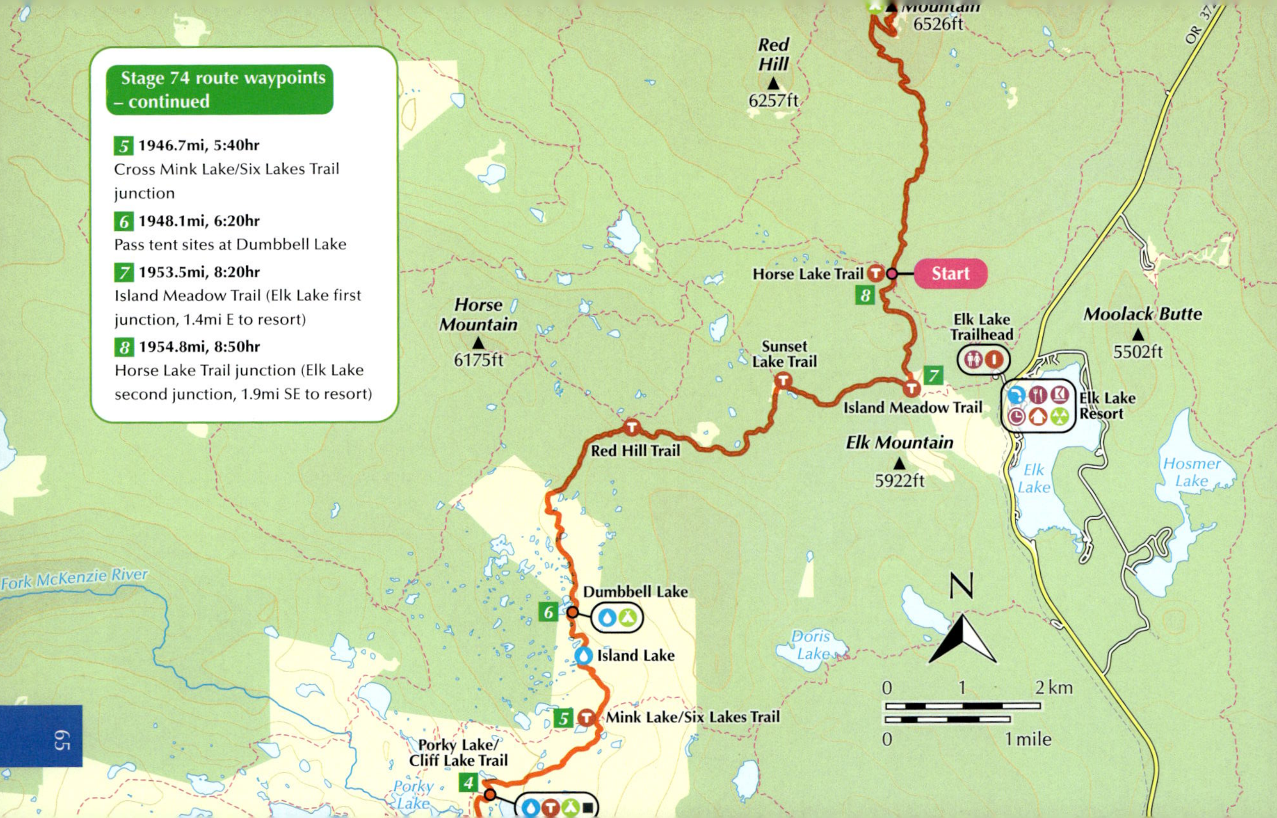

Stage 74 route waypoints – continued
5 1946.7mi, 5:40hr
Cross Mink Lake/Six Lakes Trail junction
6 1948.1mi, 6:20hr
Pass tent sites at Dumbbell Lake
7 1953.5mi, 8:20hr
Island Meadow Trail (Elk Lake first junction, 1.4mi E to resort)
8 1954.8mi, 8:50hr
Horse Lake Trail junction (Elk Lake second junction, 1.9mi SE to resort)
6526ft
Red Hill
6257ft
Horse Lake Trail
Start
Horse Mountain
6175ft
Sunset Lake Trail
Island Meadow Trail
Elk Lake Trailhead
Elk Lake Resort
Moolack Butte
5502ft
Elk Mountain
5922ft
Elk Lake
Hosmer Lake
Red Hill Trail
Fork McKenzie River
Dumbbell Lake
Island Lake
Doris Lake
Mink Lake/Six Lakes Trail
Porky Lake/ Cliff Lake Trail
Porky Lake
N
0
1
2 km
1 mile

Stage 75 route waypoints – continued

4 1972.7mi, 7:50hr
Keep R past Obsidian Falls Trail and then Glacier Way Trail

5 1977.2mi, 9:45hr
Minnie Scott spring

6 1978.2mi, 10:10hr
Keep R past Scott Trail (to McKenzie Highway Trailhead)

7 1980.6mi, 11:10hr
Keep L past Scott Pass Trail, across saddle, R past North Matthieu Lake Trail

8 1984.7mi, 12:55hr
Hwy 242 near McKenzie Pass (Sisters 15mi E, Bend 37mi SE)

You also pass through a restricted camping area at South and North Matthieu Lakes – follow local signage.

In this stage you enter the tightly controlled Obsidian Limited Entry Area (mile 1972.5 – 1974.5). PCT hikers are allowed to pass through on the PCT, but not permitted to leave the trail for approximately two miles. Camping is prohibited in this area without a special permit.

SECTION 9 – HIGHWAY 242 MCKENZIE PASS TO CASCADE LOCKS

	Stage	Distance (miles)	Total ascent (feet)	Total descent (feet)	Average duration (hr:min)	Page
76	Hwy 242 McKenzie Pass – Santiam Pass	17.1	1739	2201	7:10	73
77	Santiam Pass – Milk Creek	27.6	3737	4134	12:25	75
78	Milk Creek – Breitenbush Lake	12.2	2697	1542	6:30	77
79	Breitenbush Lake – Road 42	34.4	2851	4885	14:05	79
80	Road 42 – Barlow Pass	18.1	2001	1293	7:25	83
81	Barlow Pass – Lolo Pass	22.7	4439	5207	11:15	85
82	Lolo Pass – Wahtum Lake	16.4	2244	1768	6:40	87
83	Wahtum Lake – I-84 Cascade Locks	16.1	2005	5620	7:00	86
Totals		**164.6**	**21,713**	**26,650**	**72:30**	

WHAT TO EXPECT

As you leave McKenzie Pass behind you and head into Northern Oregon, the more recent unvegetated lava flows give way to an altogether more ancient volcanic landscape eroded from ice-age glaciation. Here these giants have settled more comfortably into the landscape and wear a forested skirt around their lower slopes; the greater precipitation creating dense, shady stands of fir and pine that thin with the increasing altitude.

There are four significant peaks passed close by the trail. First Mount Washington, Three Fingered Jack and Mount Jefferson in quick succession, then a long, forested stretch, punctuated by the shoreline of Timothy Lake, unmissable for a leisurely swim. Finally, the long, dry climb up Mount Hood where you join the Timberline Trail across the southwest slopes and tackle the glacial-fed creeks. The slopes of Mount Hood were badly affected by the Dollar Lake Fire of 2011 and it is encouraging now to see a carpet ablaze with violet fireweed among the stone grey masts that remain. After an obligatory visit to the historic Timberline Lodge (where hikers typically indulge in the 'all you can eat' buffet) it is tempting to consider a short alternate, past the spectacular Ramona Falls. Beyond, another alternate beckons that sees most hikers adopt the Eagle Creek Trail for the 3000ft descent to the Columbia River Gorge and the Bridge of the Gods.

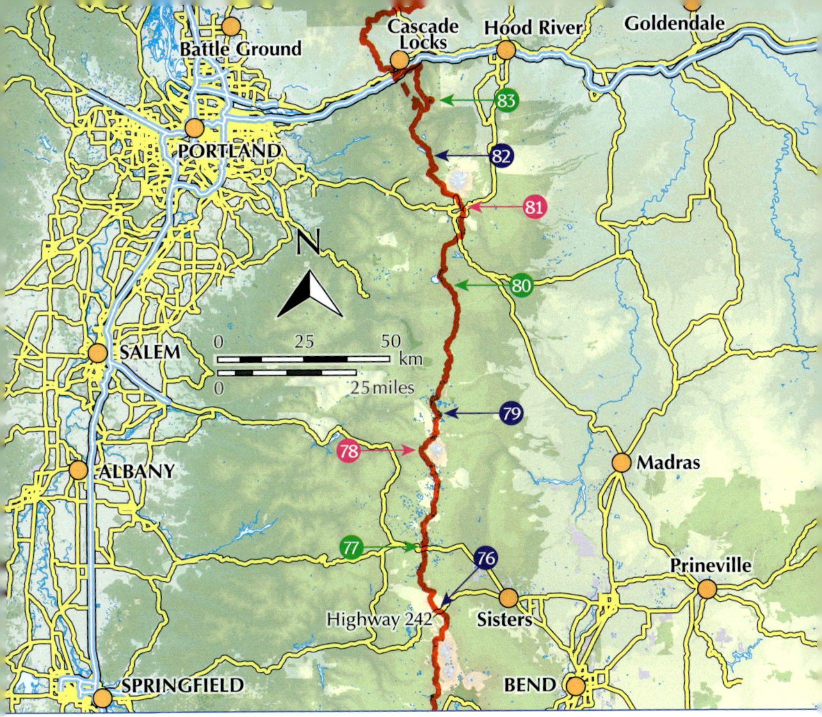

Cascade Locks
Hood River
Goldendale
Battle Ground
83
PORTLAND
82
81
N
80
0
25
50
km
0
25 miles
SALEM
79
78
ALBANY
Madras
77
76
Prineville
Highway 242
Sisters
SPRINGFIELD
BEND

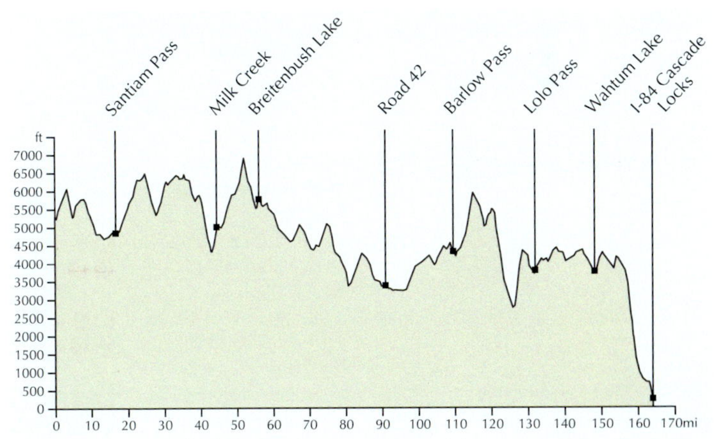

Santiam Pass
Milk Creek
Breitenbush Lake
Road 42
Barlow Pass
Lolo Pass
Wahtum Lake
I-84 Cascade Locks
ft
7000
6500
6000
5500
5000
4500
4000
3500
3000
2500
2000
1500
1000
500
0
0
10
20
30
40
50
60
70
80
90
100
110
120
130
140
150
160
170mi

This section is best hiked from mid July to September, when the flow in the glacial creeks has lessened to enable safe crossing. As ever, long stretches could face diminished water supply late in the season and local reports need to be checked. Otherwise, outside of the climb of Mount Hood, the trail provides easy going on gentle, undulating terrain, where hikers keen to reach Washington can make good time.

With the faster hiking, it is quite possible to traverse the section on a single resupply. Big Lake Youth Camp is a great place to receive a package, take stock and clean up equipment. The dedicated PCT hut with kitchen and laundry facility is a generous concession. A hitch into Government Camp is fairly easy to secure and, if not receiving a package here or at Timberline Lodge, then the store is sufficient to top up for the final stretch to Cascade Locks. Once there it is worth considering a trip out to Hood River, a beautiful and easily navigated town with good stores and an excellent outfitter, especially as the regular Columbia Area Transit bus makes the journey simple.

RESUPPLY OPTIONS

Stage	Trail mile	Place	Off trail (miles)	Description	Facilities
76	1996.1	Big Lake Youth Camp	0.8 N	Church Camp, accepts packages, kitchen, shower, camping offsite	
79	2048.2	Olallie Lake Resort	0.1 E	Small off-grid camp and cabins with small store	
80	2089.1	CJs Foodmart	1.9 NW	Chevron gas station and mini-mart with hot food deli on Hwy 26	
80	2094.1	Government Camp	5.2 W	Small ski town, several lodgings, restaurants and small store	
81	2099.6	Timberline Lodge	0.2 S	Ski resort, lodge, famous buffet and accepts packages ($)	
83	2149.3	Cascade Locks	On trail	Small town, riverside camping, bus to Portland or Hood River	
83	2149.3	Hood River	20.0 E	Larger town, bigger stores, good outfitter	

PERMITS

Permits may be required for day use and overnight trips in Mount Hood Wilderness, PCT miles 2089.2 to 2116.9 and Mark O. Hatfield Wilderness, PCT miles 2131.3 to 2145.2.

Wilderness permits are required when provided at a portal, from May 15 until October 15. Not all trails will have Wilderness portals. Permits are free and self-issued.

For more information call the Hood River Ranger District office at (541) 352-6002 or visit: www.fs.usda.gov/recarea/mthood/recarea/?recid=79439

Looking north to Mount Washington from the lava field around Belknap Crater (Stage 76)

MAIL DROP INFORMATION

'Your Name Here'
c/o Big Lake Youth Camp
26435 Big Lake Rd
Sisters, OR 97759
ETA: 'Your ETA'
Phone them on: (503) 850-3562.
Visit them at: www.biglake.org

Guest Services
Timberline Lodge
PCT Hiker 'Your name'
27500 E Timberline Rd Government Camp, OR 97028
ETA: 'Your ETA'
They are open: Mon–Sun 9am–5pm
Phone them on: (503) 272-3311
Visit them at: www.timberlinelodge.com

POST OFFICE INFORMATION

'Your Name Here'
c\o General Delivery
Government Camp, OR 97028
Located at: 88331 E Government Camp Loop
Phone them on: (503) 272-3238

'Your Name Here'
c\o General Delivery
Cascade Locks, OR 97014
Located at: 461 NW Wanapa Street
Phone them on: (541) 374-5026

'Your Name Here'
c\o General Delivery
Hood River, OR 97031
Located at: 408 Cascade Avenue
Phone them on: (541) 386-1584

Stage 76 route waypoints

1 **1984.8mi, 0:05hr**
Trailhead parking lot and Mount Washington Wilderness Boundary

2 **1987.3mi, 1:20hr**
Pass Little Belknap Trail on R then trail to main Belknap Crater on L

3 **1992.3mi, 3:40hr**
Easily missed Washington Ponds (small and stagnant) 0.1mi SW

4 **1994.7mi, 4:30hr**
Coldwater spring (small meadow hole, early–mid season)

5 **1996.1mi, 4:55hr**
Big Lake Youth Camp Trail (alternate: 0.8mi out and back, or 1.7mi loop, marked 'user trail')

6 **1998.1mi, 5:40hr**
Cross unpaved Old Santiam Road (rejoin PCT from BLYC alternate)

7 **2001.8mi, 7:10hr**
Cross Hwy 20 Santiam Pass (if hitching turn L, 200yds for wider road)

Stage 76

Highway 242 McKenzie Pass to Santiam Pass

Start	**Highway 242 McKenzie Pass**
Finish	**Santiam Pass**
Distance	**17.1 miles**
Total ascent	**1739ft**
Total descent	**2201ft**
Duration	**7:10hr**

North of McKenzie Pass you continue across the lava fields ascending the slopes of Belknap Crater. With no shade among the sun-baked rock, this can be hot. Carry plenty of water. With only two unreliable water sources on route, most will visit Big Lake Youth Camp, where a hut with kitchen and laundry has been provided for hikers. Sending a package here can avoid the need to hitch a considerable distance to Sisters or Bend for resupply.

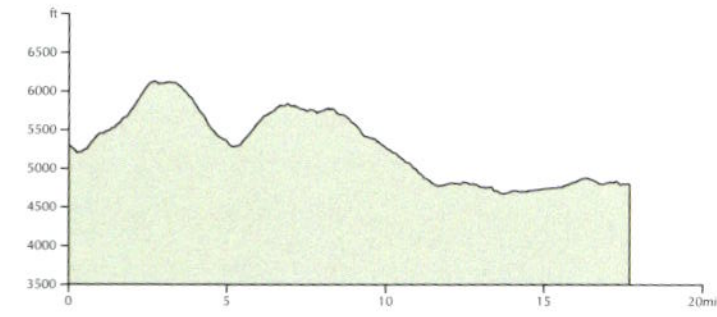

Mount Washington, Mount Thielsen, Three Fingered Jack, Mount Bailey, and Diamond Peak are known as Oregon's 'Matterhorns'. They all have a spire-like appearance, often compared to the pinnacle of the Matterhorn in Switzerland, from which the name originates.

Mount Washington
7795ft
3 Washington Ponds
Belknap Crater
2 Little Belknap Trail
1 McKenzie Pass Trailhead
Highway 242 near McKenzie Pass
8
Start
Lava Camp Lake Trailhead
Lava Camp Trail
North Matthieu Lake Trail
Harlow Crater
6216ft
242
242
Scott Mountain

Stage 77 route waypoints

1 **2002.2mi, 0:15hr**
Keep L as Old Summit Trail forks R

2 **2003.2mi, 0:45hr**
Bear R as Santiam Lake Trail departs L (useful bad weather alternate)

3 **2009.3mi, 3:50hr**
Porcupine Peak saddle, North Ridge Three Fingered Jack

4 **2012.6mi, 5:00hr**
Keep ahead across Minto Pass/Wasco Lake Trail junction

5 **2016.5mi, 7:00hr**
Keep L past Rockpile Lake and Rockpile Trail

6 **2022.7mi, 9:50hr**
Turn R approaching saddle, head NE, past Hunts Creek Trail (S) on L

7 **2024.4mi, 10:45hr**
Shale Lake (Restricted Camping Area – follow local signs)

8 **2029.4mi, 12:25hr**
Ford Milk Crk

Milk Creek and Russell Creek ahead are both glacier-fed and can be serious crossings in early season or a wetter year. They will tend to carry less water in the morning after cooler temperatures overnight reduce run-off, water levels then rise in the afternoon as the sun increases the rate of melting. Whitewater Creek, fortunately, has a bridge. It is also extremely difficult to filter this water for drinking. The fine silt content will merely block filters.

Stage 77

Santiam Pass to Milk Creek

Start	Santiam Pass
Finish	Milk Creek
Distance	27.6 miles
Total ascent	3737ft
Total descent	4134ft
Duration	12:25hr

Water is again in short supply here, as you largely traverse ridgelines, the exception being a couple of useful lake visits. Water at these can be stagnant so ensure you filter or treat these sources. You'll also walk through an extensive burn area that dates from 2003. A lot of the dead, standing trees were brought down by the record snows of winter 2022–23, but in places some new growth is emerging.

Stage 78 route waypoints

1 **2031.0mi, 0:45hr**
Keep R past Woodpecker Ridge Trail (1.6mi W to trailhead)

2 **2032.1mi, 1:20hr**
Cross seasonal Jeff Creek (non-glacial)

3 **2033.8mi, 2:00hr**
Russell Crk, safer crossing usually found 100–150yds upstream of trail

4 **2035.9mi, 3:15hr**
Keep R past South Breitenbush Trail, across Russell Lake outlet

5 **2041.6mi, 6:30hr**
Unpaved FS Road 4220 (Breitenbush Lake and Campground 0.3mi NE)

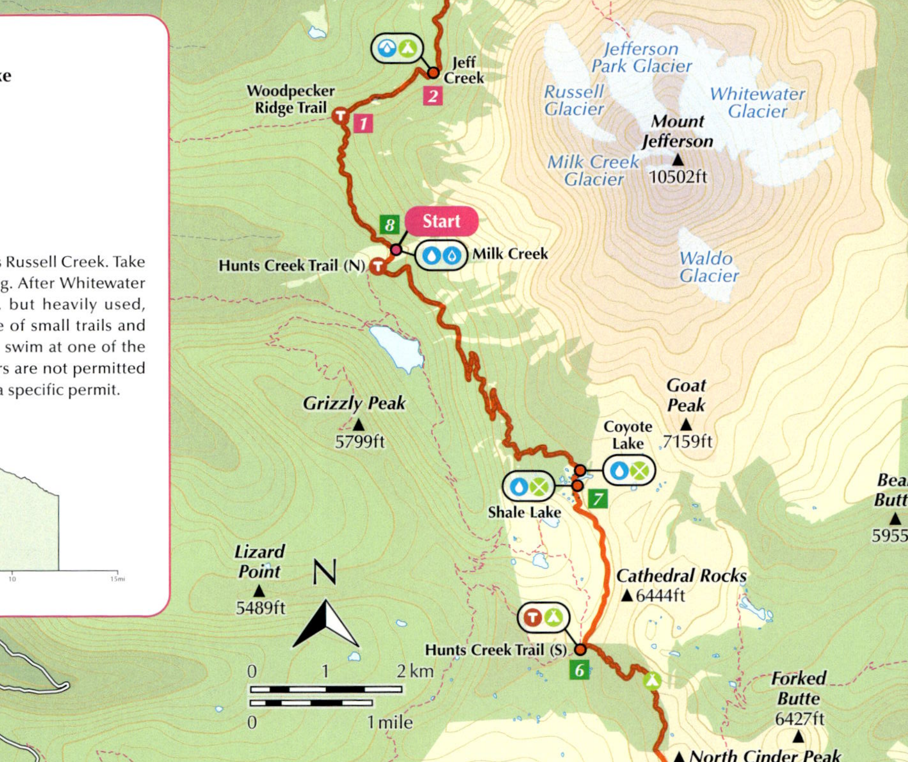

Stage 78

Milk Creek to Breitenbush Lake

Start	**Mill Creek**
Finish	**Breitenbush Lake**
Distance	**12.2 miles**
Total ascent	**2697ft**
Total descent	**1542ft**
Duration	**6:30hr**

The main challenge of the stage is Russell Creek. Take your time and find a safe crossing. After Whitewater Creek you enter the beautiful, but heavily used, Jefferson Park with its multitude of small trails and lakes. You may want to stop and swim at one of the lakes but note that the PCT hikers are not permitted to camp within the park without a specific permit.

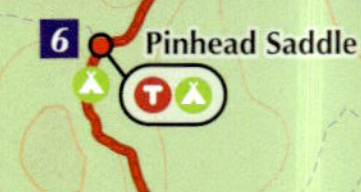

Stage 79 route waypoints

1 2043.5mi, 1:00hr
Keep L past Gibson Lake and Horseshoe Saddle Trails

2 2046.6mi, 1:55hr
Pass Cigar Lake then cross Red Lake Trail

3 2048.2mi, 2:35hr
Trail to Ollalie Lake Resort near Head Lake (0.1mi E)

4 2051.7mi, 4:00hr
Keep ahead across Russ Lake Trail

5 2057.2mi, 6:20hr
Cross Lemti Crk, if dry trail to Trooper Spring 0.1mi beyond

6 2060.9mi, 7:50hr
Pinhead Saddle and trail junction

So close to the trail, the friendly Olallie Lake Resort is worth a visit. Dating from the 1930s, its remote location means no electricity, cell coverage or Wi-Fi. In most ways it has changed very little. Just 10 cabins, tent sites and kerosene lanterns at night. There is no mail service, so no packages, but the tiny store holds some useful resupply items and often, gas canisters (cash payment only).

Stage 79

Breitenbush Lake to Road 42 (near Clackamas Lake)

Start	**Breitenbush Lake**
Finish	**Road 42 (near Clackamas Lake)**
Distance	**34.4 miles**
Total ascent	**2851ft**
Total descent	**4885ft**
Duration	**14:05hr**

A little way into this stage, at Russ Lake Trail junction, you enter the Warm Springs Indian Reservation. For next 23 miles northbound you are required to remain on the PCT right-of-way, which is 200ft wide of the trail centreline. Just before Clackamas Lake you enter Mount Hood National Forest and exit the Warm Springs Reservation.

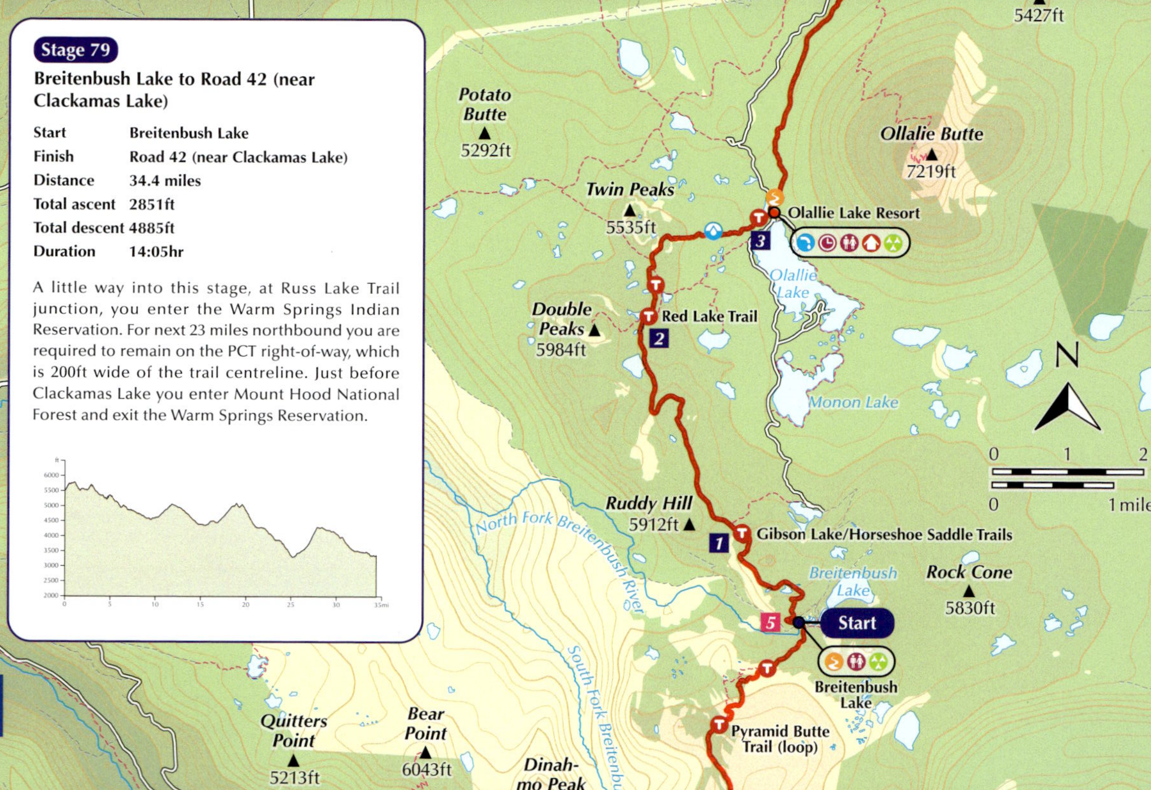

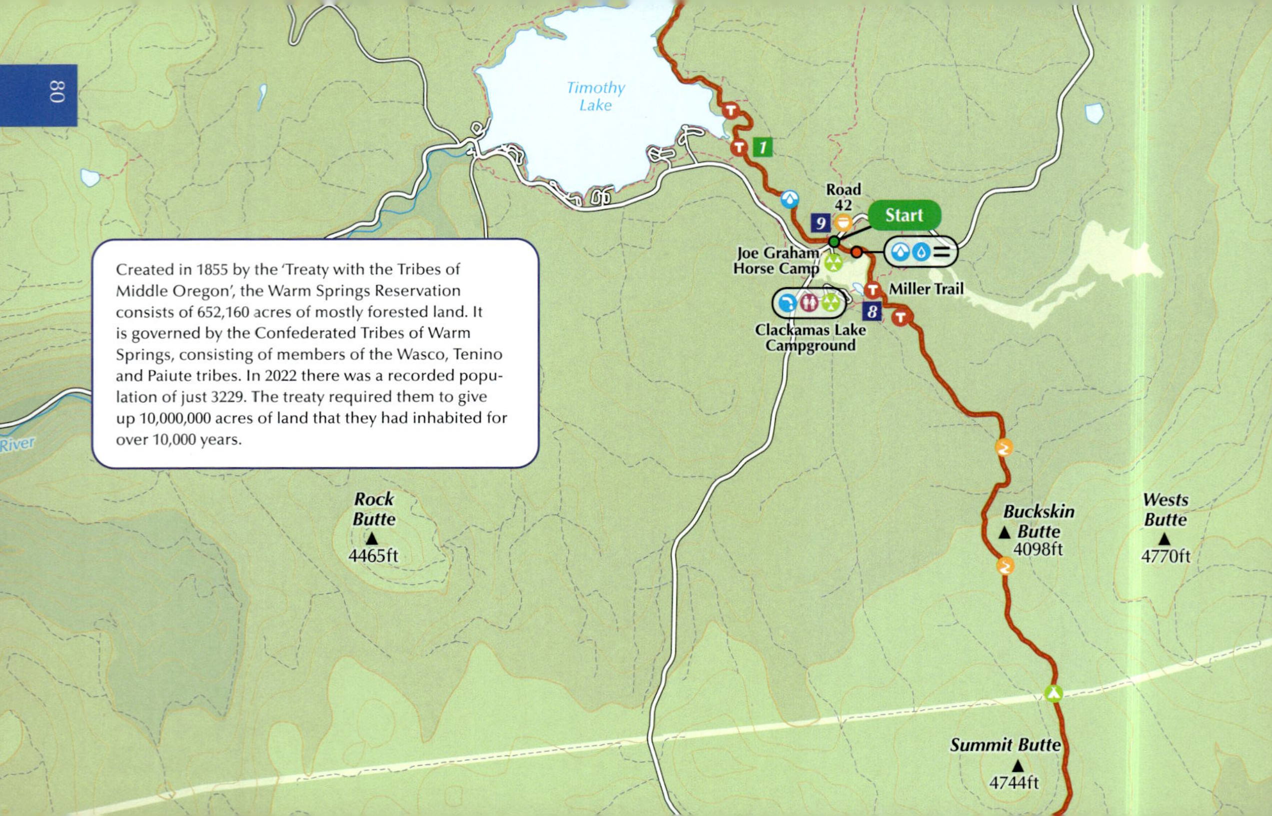

Created in 1855 by the 'Treaty with the Tribes of Middle Oregon', the Warm Springs Reservation consists of 652,160 acres of mostly forested land. It is governed by the Confederated Tribes of Warm Springs, consisting of members of the Wasco, Tenino and Paiute tribes. In 2022 there was a recorded population of just 3229. The treaty required them to give up 10,000,000 acres of land that they had inhabited for over 10,000 years.

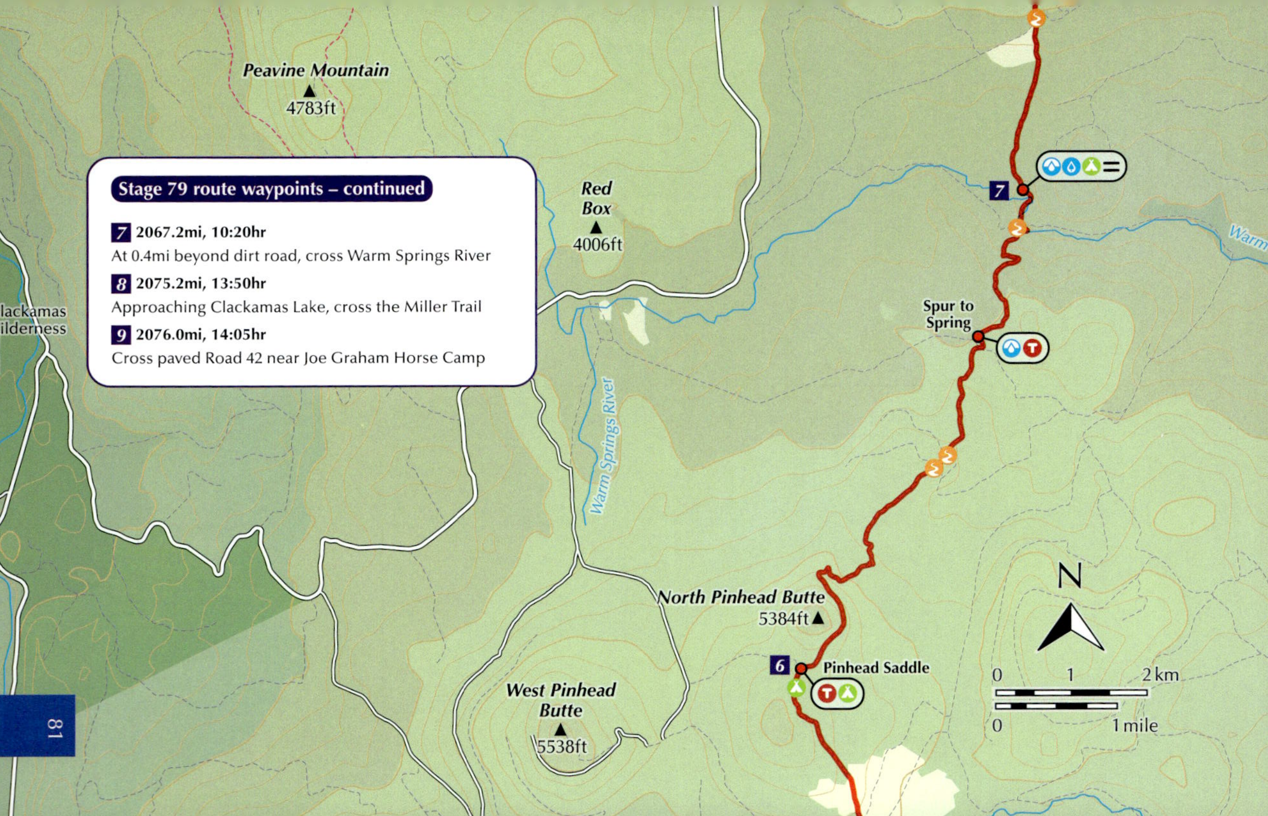

Stage 79 route waypoints – continued

7 2067.2mi, 10:20hr
At 0.4mi beyond dirt road, cross Warm Springs River

8 2075.2mi, 13:50hr
Approaching Clackamas Lake, cross the Miller Trail

9 2076.0mi, 14:05hr
Cross paved Road 42 near Joe Graham Horse Camp

Stage 80 route waypoints

1 **2077.3mi, 0:30hr**
Pass Timothy Lake Trail which circles the W lakeside

2 **2081.5mi, 1:55hr**
Little Crater Lake and Campground trail junction (lake 0.25mi E)

3 **2085.3mi, 3:50hr**
Just beyond FS Road 240, small tent site and seasonal spring on R

4 **2089.1mi, 5:20hr**
Cross Hwy 26 Wapinitia Pass and Frog Lake Trailhead (CJ's Foodmart and gas station is 1.9 miles NW), Frog Lake Campground 0.6mi S with well water

5 **2094.1mi, 7:25hr**
Barlow Pass, just S of Hwy 35 (Government Camp 5.2mi W)

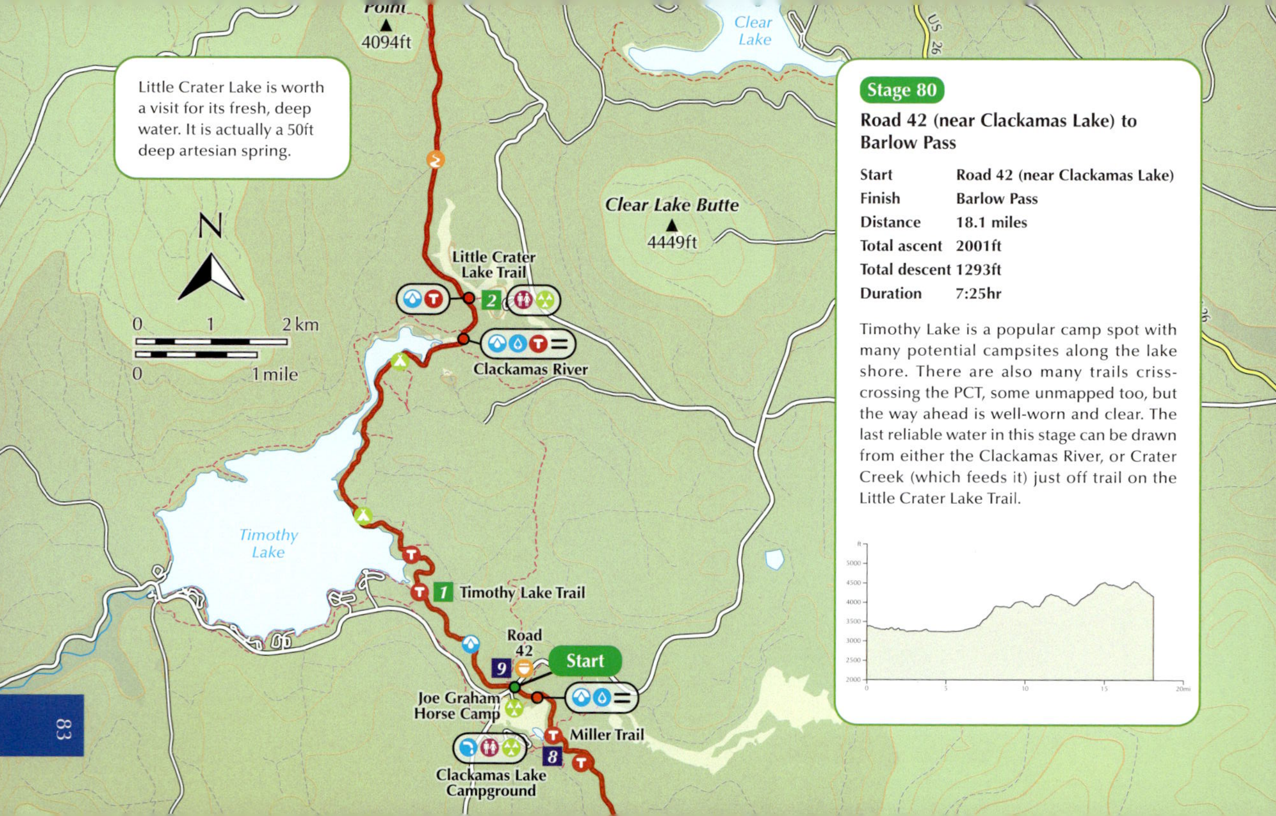

Little Crater Lake is worth a visit for its fresh, deep water. It is actually a 50ft deep artesian spring.

Stage 80

Road 42 (near Clackamas Lake) to Barlow Pass

Start	**Road 42 (near Clackamas Lake)**
Finish	**Barlow Pass**
Distance	**18.1 miles**
Total ascent	**2001ft**
Total descent	**1293ft**
Duration	**7:25hr**

Timothy Lake is a popular camp spot with many potential campsites along the lake shore. There are also many trails criss-crossing the PCT, some unmapped too, but the way ahead is well-worn and clear. The last reliable water in this stage can be drawn from either the Clackamas River, or Crater Creek (which feeds it) just off trail on the Little Crater Lake Trail.

Stage 81 route waypoints

1 2097.1mi, 1:20hr
Small spring and tent sites

2 2099.6mi, 3:00hr
Trail to Timberline Lodge (0.2mi S)

3 2102.9mi, 4:20hr
Cross the silty Zigzag River (challenging early season)

4 2105.3mi, 5:50hr
Rushing Water Crk (headwaters may be below boulders)

5 2109.0mi, 7:15hr
Ford Sandy River (with care, can be dangerous, a hiker died here in 2004)

6 2109.5mi, 7:25hr
Ramona Falls Trail on R is a highly recommended alternate

7 2111.0mi, 8:00hr
Turn R (NE) at Sandy River Trail junction (Ramona Falls Trail rejoins in 0.5mi)

8 2114.0mi, 10:10hr
Follow ridge NW from Timberline/Top Spur Trail junction

9 2116.8mi, 11:15hr
Cross unpaved road at Lolo Pass Trailhead

Built and furnished by local artisans during the Great Depression as part of the 'New Deal', Timberline Lodge (6000ft) is a National Historic Landmark, dedicated in 1937 by President Franklin D. Roosevelt. For many of course, it is most famous as the exterior of the Overlook Hotel in Stanley Kubrick's 1980s classic, *The Shining*, starring a young Jack Nicholson.

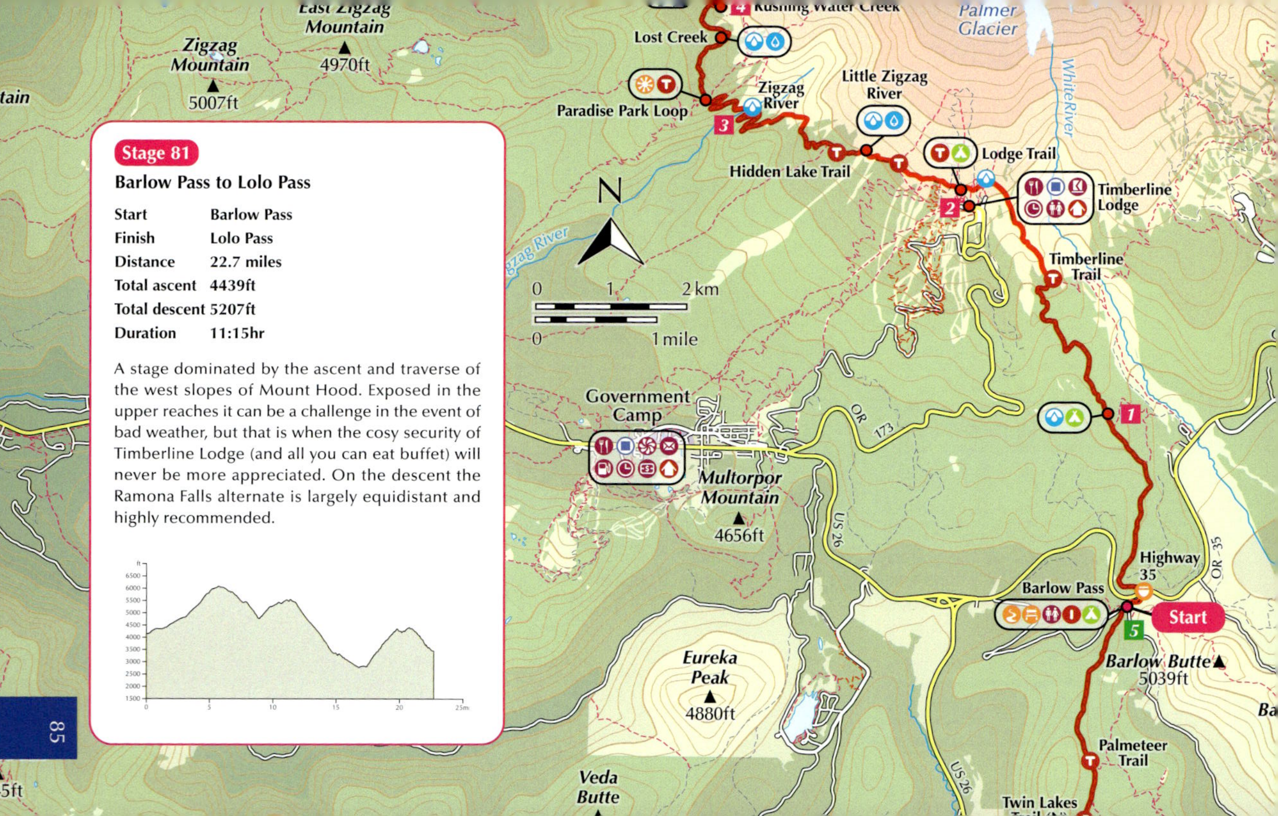

Stage 81

Barlow Pass to Lolo Pass

Start	Barlow Pass
Finish	Lolo Pass
Distance	22.7 miles
Total ascent	4439ft
Total descent	5207ft
Duration	11:15hr

A stage dominated by the ascent and traverse of the west slopes of Mount Hood. Exposed in the upper reaches it can be a challenge in the event of bad weather, but that is when the cosy security of Timberline Lodge (and all you can eat buffet) will never be more appreciated. On the descent the Ramona Falls alternate is largely equidistant and highly recommended.

Stage 83

Wahtum Lake to Interstate 84 Cascade Locks

Start	Wahtum Lake
Finish	Interstate 84 Cascade Locks
Distance	16.1 miles
Total ascent	2005ft
Total descent	5620ft
Duration	7:00hr

Effectively the 'equestrian alternative' to the Eagle Creek Trail, this is nonetheless a beautiful route, descending a ridgeline in the Mark O. Hatfield Wilderness area, before turning west into the Columbia River Gorge National Scenic Area, with glimpses of the river.

Stage 83 route waypoints

1 2134.9mi, 0:40hr
Bear L past Herman Creek Trail, the ahead past Chinidere Cutoff (L) and Mountain (R) Trails

2 2138.0mi, 2:00hr
The Eagle-Benson Trail connects to the Eagle Creek Trail. Several subsequent trails lead L to Ruckel Creek and Benson Camp

Stage 82

Lolo Pass to Wahtum Lake

Start	Lolo Pass
Finish	Wahtum Lake
Distance	16.4 miles
Total ascent	2244ft
Total descent	1768ft
Duration	6:40hr

A short, forested stage with limited water and few camping opportunities on trail. Most hikers will take the recommended scenic alternate route 14.3 miles from Indian Springs Trail, adjoining the Eagle Creek Trail, to rejoin the PCT just before the Bridge of the Gods at Cascade Locks.

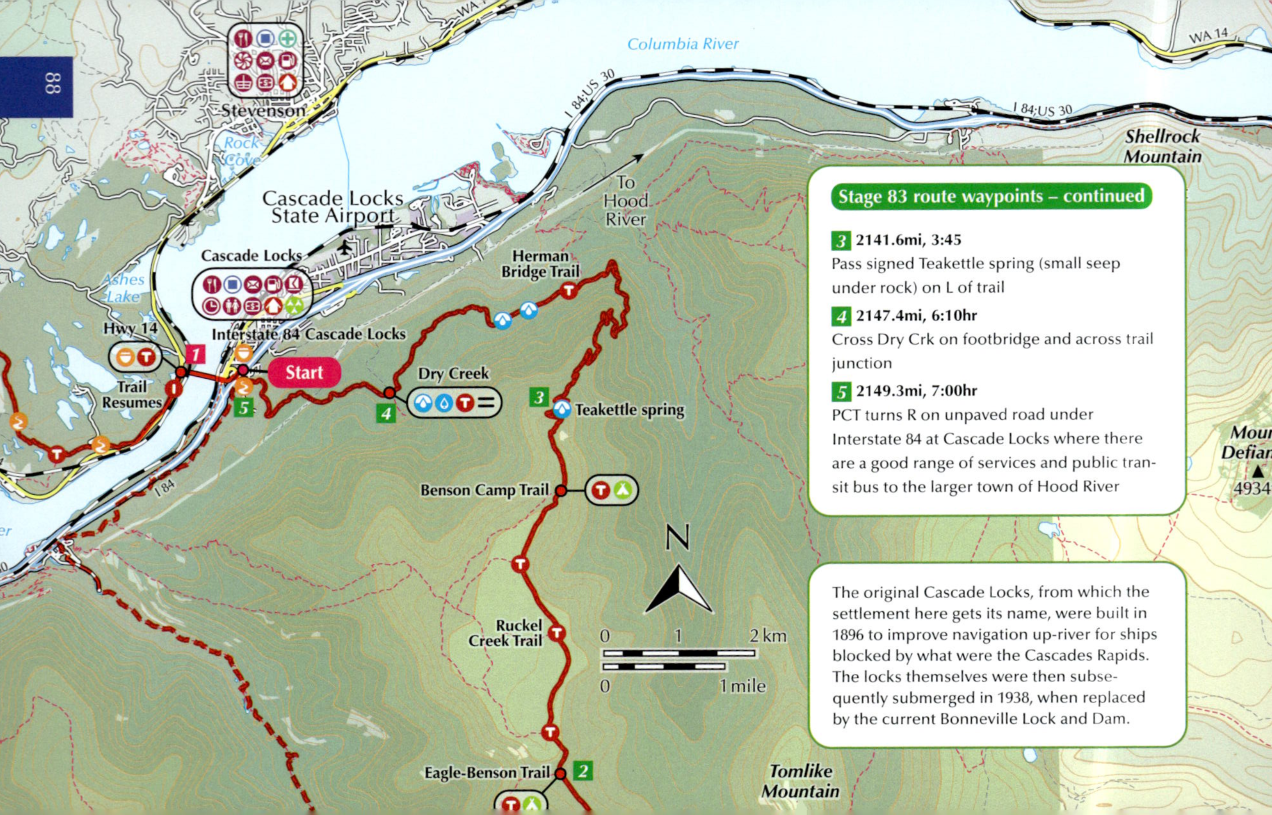

Stage 83 route waypoints – continued

3 2141.6mi, 3:45
Pass signed Teakettle spring (small seep under rock) on L of trail

4 2147.4mi, 6:10hr
Cross Dry Crk on footbridge and across trail junction

5 2149.3mi, 7:00hr
PCT turns R on unpaved road under Interstate 84 at Cascade Locks where there are a good range of services and public transit bus to the larger town of Hood River

The original Cascade Locks, from which the settlement here gets its name, were built in 1896 to improve navigation up-river for ships blocked by what were the Cascades Rapids. The locks themselves were then subsequently submerged in 1938, when replaced by the current Bonneville Lock and Dam.

SECTION 10 – INTERSTATE 84 CASCADE LOCKS INTERSTATE 90 TO SNOQUALMIE PASS

	Stage	Distance	Total ascent (feet)	Total descent (feet)	Average duration (hr:min)	Page
84	I-84 Cascade Locks – Wind River Rd	33.3	6447	5571	15:55	95
85	Wind River Rd – Road 24	34.8	6152	2999	16:00	97
86	Road 24 – Road 23	14.1	1808	2159	6:15	101
87	Road 23 – Road 5603	22.2	3038	2198	10:20	102
88	Road 5603 – Hwy 12 near White Pass	43.8	6709	7116	21:15	105
89	Hwy 12 near White Pass – Chinook Pass	28.6	4580	3550	14:45	106
90	Chinook Pass – Road 784	32	4327	4833	13:50	111
91	Road 784 – Stampede Pass	19.4	3383	4626	8:30	112
92	Stampede Pass – I-90 Snoqualmie Pass	18.3	3268	3973	8:20	115
Totals		**246.5**	**39,712**	**37,025**	**115:10**	

WHAT TO EXPECT

The Columbia River Forest is a lush, damp and moss-strewn environment through which the trail winds its way upward on viewless slopes. Leaving behind the PCT's lowest point, 99ft just before the climb up to the toll booth on the Bridge of the Gods, Washington truly feels like a new region. Entering Indian Heaven Wilderness you find a forested, volcanic plateau, the skyline dominated by Lemei Rock, the highest point in the wilderness and a shield volcano topped by cinder cones and spatter cones. The rich volcanic soils here support an impressive array of wildflowers which, along with the more than 150 lakes, ensure a thriving population of biting insects in the initial weeks after the snow melt.

Circling Mount Adams, especially during the fall, you are likely to share tent sites with grazing deer and elk, and at night your dreams are accompanied by the creaking of ice on the glaciers above. Climbing to the Packwood Glacier, below Old Snowy Mountain, the view of the notorious Goat Rocks opens up, a line of impossible looking spires, that belie the notion of a trail across them. Yet traverse them it does, switching back and forth on rocks rich in color, from deep reds to yellows and browns. Beyond it is hard

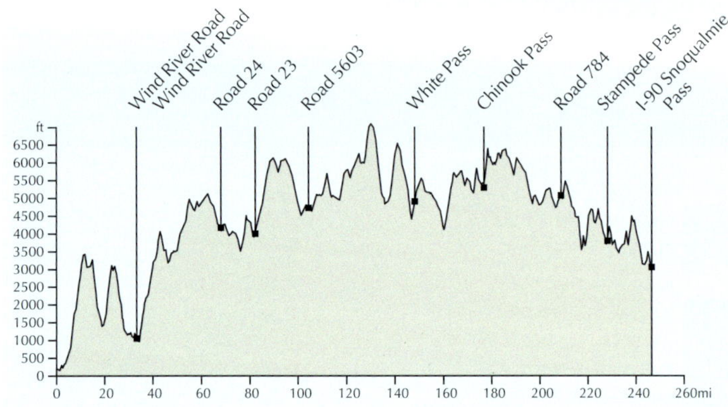

not to be mesmerized by the white-topped outline of Mount Rainier, but the focus here must be on foot placement to ensure a safe crossing.

Beyond White Pass the trail crosses a plateau, dotted with pools and lakes, and rich in wildflowers. Climbing once again the trail hugs the watershed and veers from saddle to saddle between descriptively named peaks such as Crown Point, Castle Mountain and Pyramid Peak. After so much natural beauty, the descent into Snoqualmie Pass can be a little underwhelming, through swathes of old clear-cut felling and below the infrastructure of a modern ski resort. Nonetheless, after the 100-mile stretch from White Pass, most will welcome the handful of cafés and stores, and the hospitality of the Washington Alpine Club hut is nothing short of legendry.

Timing for this section is highly dependent on the snowmelt. In most years it will be accessible by mid July. Goat Rocks is not somewhere to be in the snow without being fully prepared. Resupply here has in the past been largely dependent on sending a package to either the Summit Inn or the Chevron gas station. More recently Lee's Summit Grocery at Snoqualmie appear to be stocking hiker-focused resupply items and it could be possible to put together a basic resupply between here and the Chevron. Similarly in Trout Lake and White Pass, local businesses are working hard to respond to hiker needs and it is good to support these small stores whenever possible.

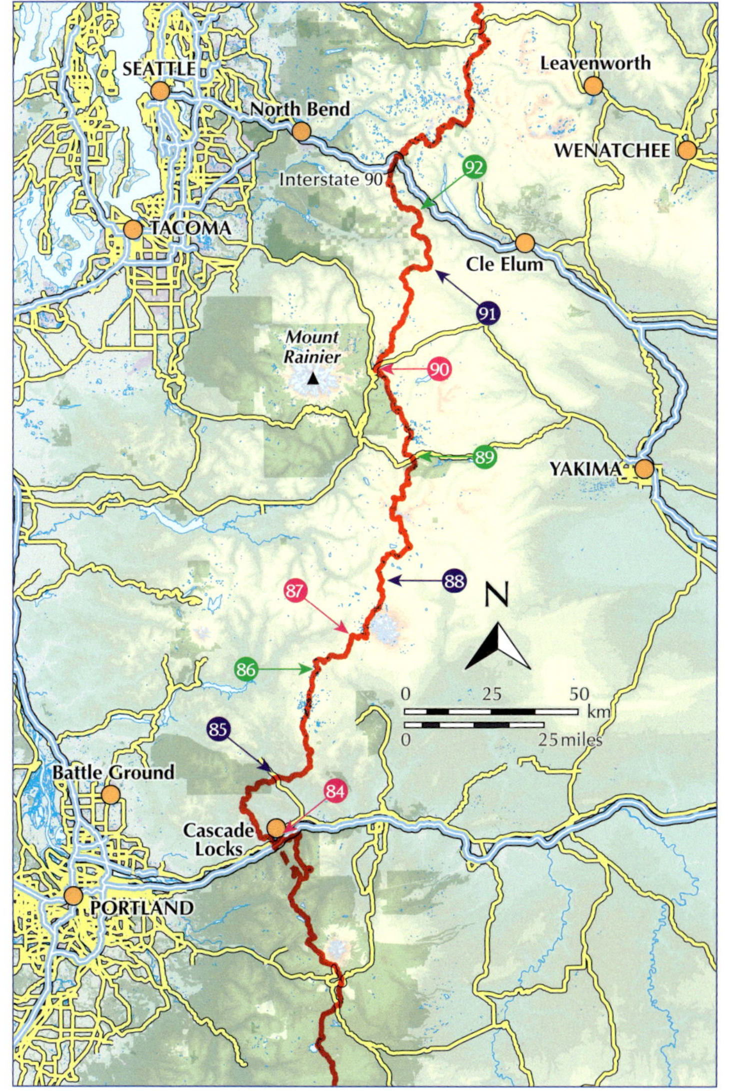
SEATTLE
North Bend
Leavenworth
WENATCHEE
Interstate 90
92
TACOMA
Cle Elum
91
Mount Rainier
90
89
YAKIMA
88
87
N
86
0
25
50
km
0
25 miles
85
Battle Ground
84
Cascade Locks
PORTLAND

RESUPPLY OPTIONS

Stage	Trail mile	Place	Off trail (miles)	Description	Facilities
84	2149.9	Stevenson	3.0 NE	Small town N of Columbia River, good market, hardware store	
86	2231.5	Trout Lake	13.8 S	Great trail angels, store w/ camping, showers, laundry, accepts packages	
88	2297.5	White Pass	0.5 W	Kracker Barrel gas/store, hiker friendly, most services, accept packages ($)	
88	2297.5	Packwood	20.5 W	Small town, good food market	
92	2395.8	Snoqualmie Pass	On trail	Summit Inn and Chevron (PO) accept packages, WAC Hut/Lodge nearby	

PERMITS

Permits are required for day use and overnight trips in Indian Heaven Wilderness, PCT miles 2203.2 to 2216.2, Mount Adams Wilderness, PCT miles 2233.6 to 2252.5, Goat Rocks Wilderness, PCT miles 2260.1 to 2295.5, William O'Douglas Wilderness, PCT miles 2298.8 to 2315.5, Mount Rainier Wilderness, PCT miles 2298.8 to 2315.5, and Norse Peak Wilderness, PCT miles 2335.8 to 2348.9

Indian Heaven Wilderness/Mount Adams Wilderness/Goat Rocks Wilderness

Wilderness permits are required for day use and overnight use in all Gifford Pinchot National Forest Wildernesses. The self-issued permits are free and are available at all trailheads leading into these Wildernesses, and at Forest Service Ranger Stations.

For more information call the Mount Adams Ranger District office at (509) 395-3402 or visit: www.fs.usda.gov/recarea/giffordpinchot/recarea/?recid=79410

The ridgeline of Goat Rocks is a truly spectacular traverse in good weather (Stage 88)

William O'Douglas Wilderness

Wilderness permits are required for day and overnight use. The self-issued permits are free and are available at trailheads and Forest Service Ranger Stations.

For more information call the Naches Ranger District office at (509) 653-1401 or visit: www.fs.usda.gov/recarea/okawen/recarea/?recid=79426

Mount Rainier Wilderness

Wilderness permits are required for overnight use. Reservations are encouraged but not required. Two thirds of the available quota are made available in advance for reservation with a lottery operating for early access in February, the remainder becoming available for reservation in April. The remaining one third are available on a walk-up basis up to one day before your trip from Wilderness Information Centers.

To obtain a permit visit: www.recreation.gov/permits/4675317

For more information call the Wilderness Information Center at (360) 569-6650 or visit: www.nps.gov/mora/planyourvisit/wilderness-permit.htm

Norse Peak Wilderness

Wilderness permits are required for day use and overnight use in all Okanogan-Wenatchee Wildernesses. The self-issued permits are free and are available at all trailheads leading into these Wildernesses, and at Forest Service Ranger Stations.

For more information call the Naches Ranger District office at (509) 653-1401 or visit: www.fs.usda.gov/detail/okawen/passes-permits/?cid=fsbdev3_053610#norse%20peak

The Bridge of the Gods at the Oregon/Washington border (Stage 84)

MAIL DROP INFORMATION

Trout Lake
'Your Name' – 'ETA: m/d'
c/o Trout Lake Grocery
PO Box 132
Trout Lake, WA 98650
They are open: 7:30am–7pm
Phone them on: (509) 395-2777
Visit them at: https://troutlake.org/trout-lake-grocery
Also visit: https://troutlake.org/pct-trail-angels

White Pass
'Your Name Here'
c/o the Kracker Barrel Store
48851 US Highway 12
Naches, WA 98937
They are open: 8am–6pm
Phone them on: (509) 672-3105

Summit Inn Snoqualmie
'Your Name Here'
c/o Summit Inn
603 State Route 906
Snoqualmie Pass, WA 98068
ETA: 'Your ETA'
Phone them on: (425) 434-6300
Visit them at:
www.summitinnwashington.com

POST OFFICE INFORMATION

'Your Name Here'
c\o General Delivery
Stevenson, WA 98648
Located at: 90 SW Russell Avenue
Phone them on: (509) 427-5532

'Your Name Here'
c\o General Delivery
Trout Lake, WA 98650
Located at: 2393 Highway 141
Phone them on: (509) 395-2108

'Your Name Here'
c\o General Delivery
Packwood, WA 98361
Located at: 111 Smith Road
Phone them on: (360) 494-6311

Snoqualmie Pass
Pacific Crest Trail Hiker
'Your Name Here'
ETA (month/day/year)
c/o General Delivery
Snoqualmie Pass, WA 98068
(The post office is located at the Chevron gas station).
They are open: 6am–10pm

Stage 84

Interstate 84 Cascade Locks to Wind River Road

Start	Interstate 84 Cascade Locks
Finish	Wind River Road
Distance	33.3 miles
Total ascent	6447ft
Total descent	5571ft
Duration	15:55hr

This undulating stage close to the Columbia River Gorge is a popular recreation area and there are multiple unmapped dirt tracks so navigational care is required. Shade is plentiful but be aware that there is an 11.5 mile dry stretch between Cedar and Rock Creeks. Take care crossing the Bridge of the Gods across the Columbia River. There is no sidewalk for pedestrians, and some find the metal grid unnerving to walk on, with a view between your feet to the water far below!

Stage 84 route waypoints

1 2149.9mi, 0:10hr
From bridge turn L on Hwy 14, 100yds past small lake, trail resumes on R (Stevenson 3mi NE)

2 2153.5mi, 1:40hr
Bridge Gillette Lake outflow, several trails to lake/campsites close by

3 2157.3mi, 4:00hr
Seasonal tributary of Cedar Crk

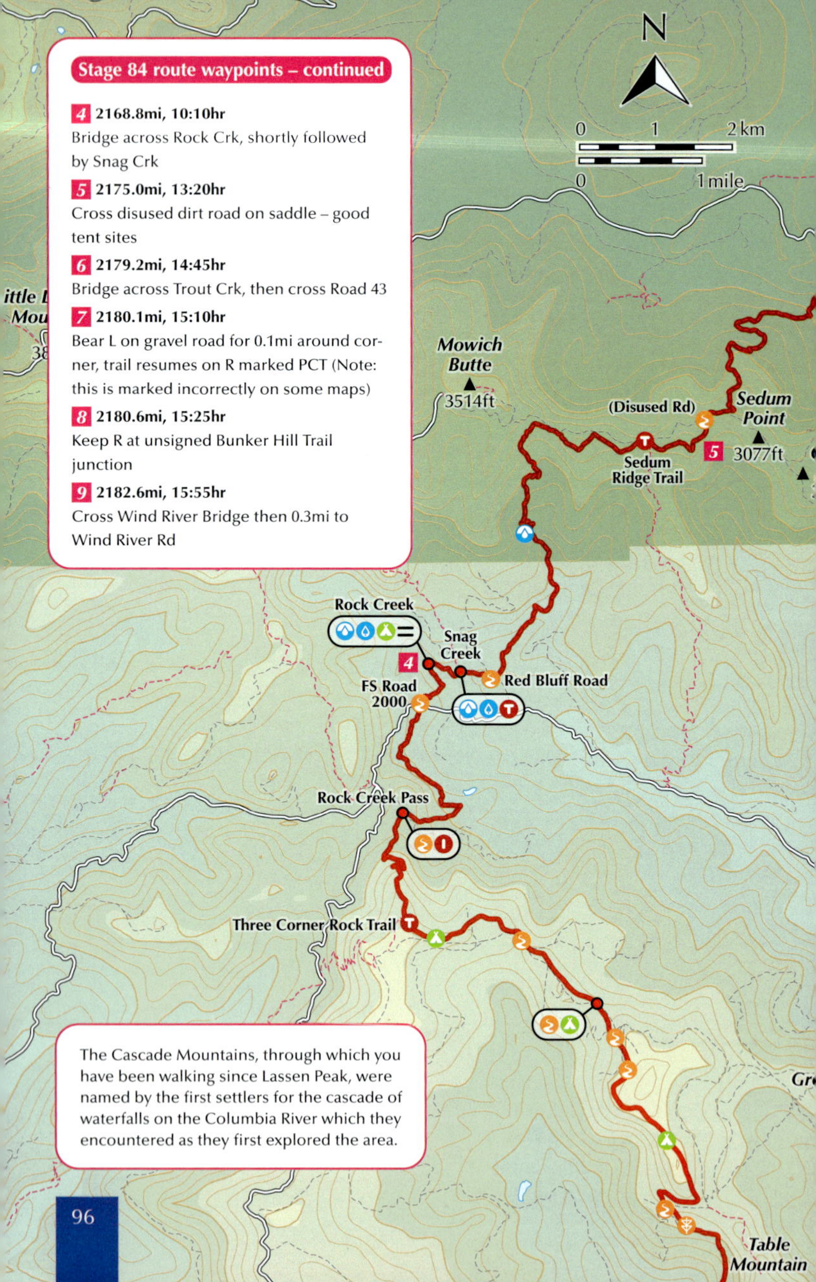

Stage 84 route waypoints – continued

4 2168.8mi, 10:10hr
Bridge across Rock Crk, shortly followed by Snag Crk

5 2175.0mi, 13:20hr
Cross disused dirt road on saddle – good tent sites

6 2179.2mi, 14:45hr
Bridge across Trout Crk, then cross Road 43

7 2180.1mi, 15:10hr
Bear L on gravel road for 0.1mi around corner, trail resumes on R marked PCT (Note: this is marked incorrectly on some maps)

8 2180.6mi, 15:25hr
Keep R at unsigned Bunker Hill Trail junction

9 2182.6mi, 15:55hr
Cross Wind River Bridge then 0.3mi to Wind River Rd

The Cascade Mountains, through which you have been walking since Lassen Peak, were named by the first settlers for the cascade of waterfalls on the Columbia River which they encountered as they first explored the area.

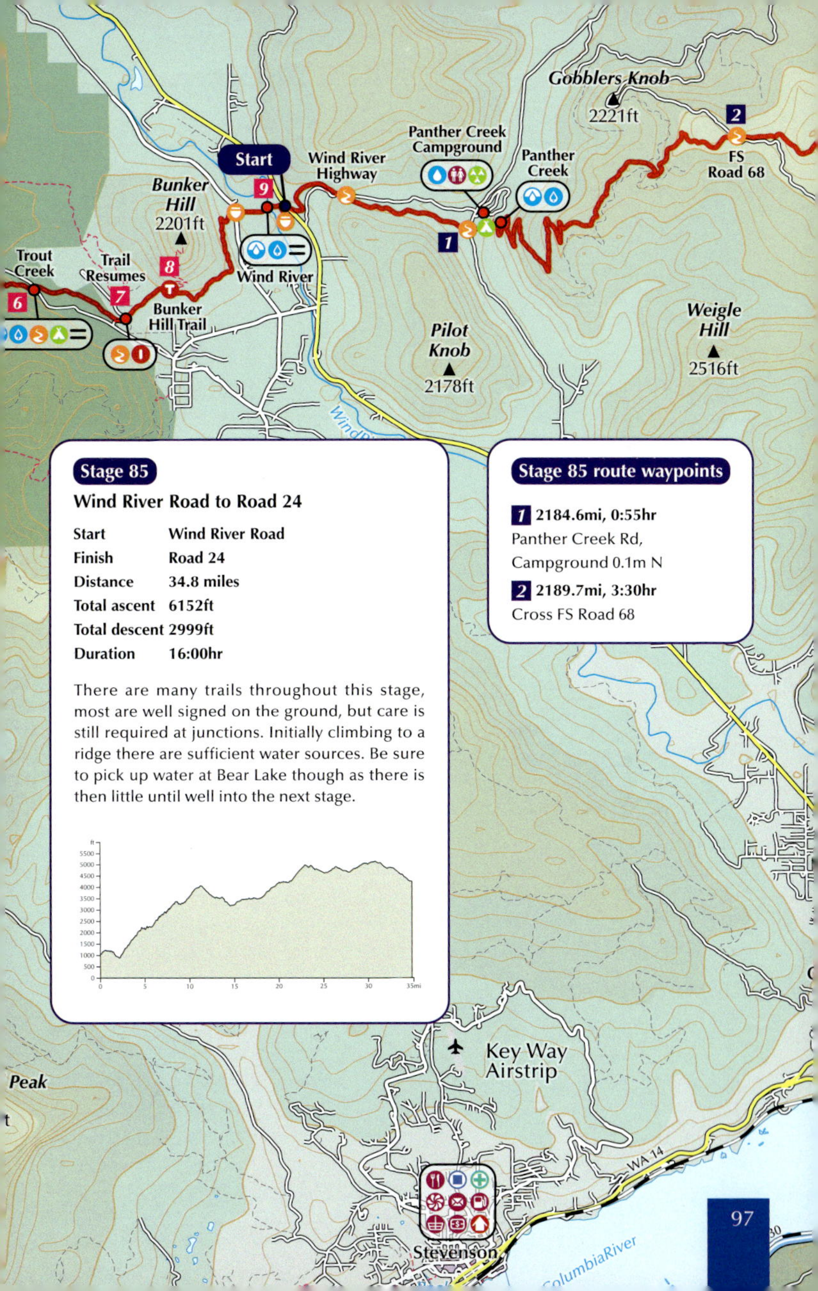

Stage 85

Wind River Road to Road 24

Start	**Wind River Road**
Finish	**Road 24**
Distance	**34.8 miles**
Total ascent	**6152ft**
Total descent	**2999ft**
Duration	**16:00hr**

There are many trails throughout this stage, most are well signed on the ground, but care is still required at junctions. Initially climbing to a ridge there are sufficient water sources. Be sure to pick up water at Bear Lake though as there is then little until well into the next stage.

Stage 85 route waypoints

1 2184.6mi, 0:55hr
Panther Creek Rd, Campground 0.1m N

2 2189.7mi, 3:30hr
Cross FS Road 68

Stage 85 route waypoints – continued

3 2192.7mi, 4:50hr
Pass Cedar Creek Trail on R

4 2195.7mi, 6:10hr
Unreliable stream and tent sites, small trail to spring

5 2200.6mi, 8:40hr
Pass through Crest Horse Camp at FS Road 60

6 2207.9mi, 11:50hr
Blue Lake, pass Tombstone Lake Trail on R, Thomas Lake Trail R at fork

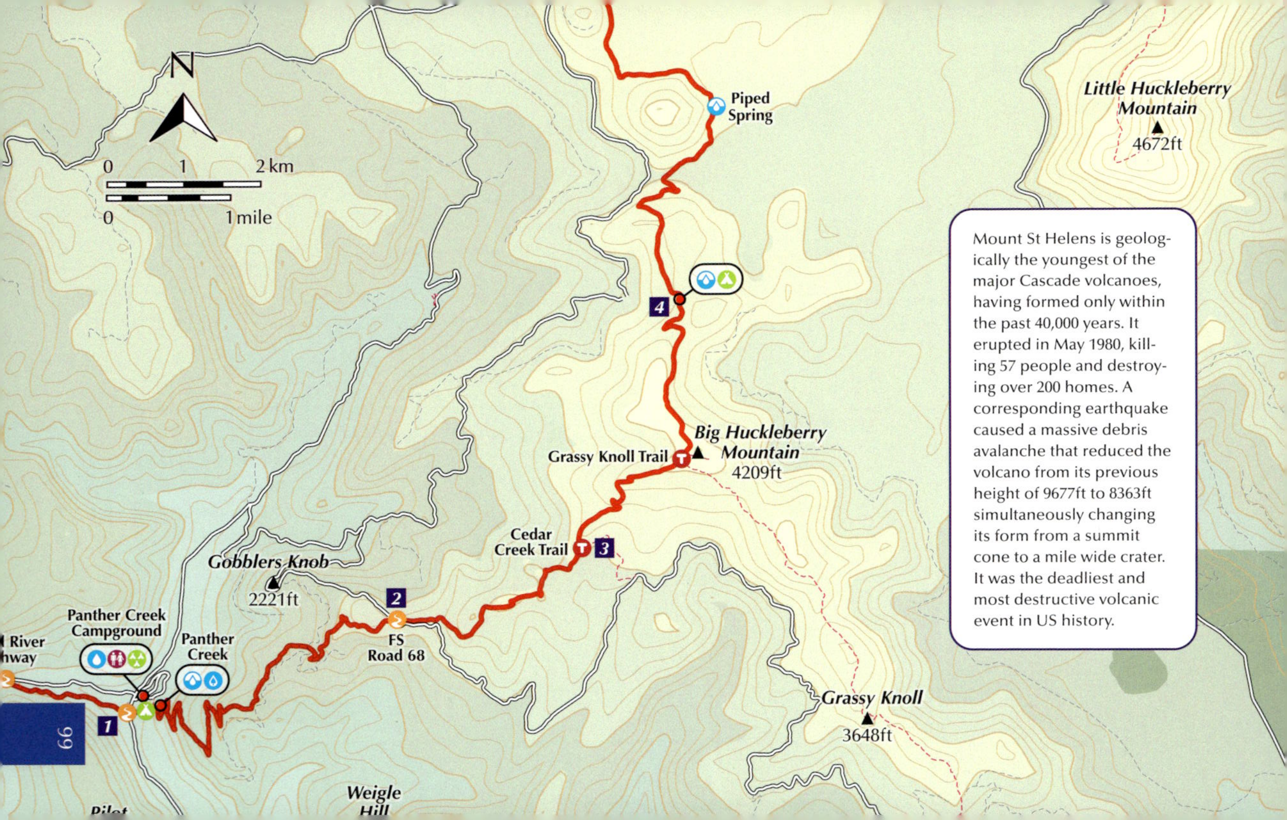

Mount St Helens is geologically the youngest of the major Cascade volcanoes, having formed only within the past 40,000 years. It erupted in May 1980, killing 57 people and destroying over 200 homes. A corresponding earthquake caused a massive debris avalanche that reduced the volcano from its previous height of 9677ft to 8363ft simultaneously changing its form from a summit cone to a mile wide crater. It was the deadliest and most destructive volcanic event in US history.

Stage 86 route waypoints
1 2221.1mi, 1:30hr
Cross FS Road 8851 and shortly after Mosquito Crk
2 2224mi, 2:40hr
Keep R passing Steamboat Lake Trail (tent sites on lake's E shore)
3 2226mi, 3:25hr
At paved FS Road 88 turn L a short way, then trail resumes R
4 2228.3mi, 4:50hr
Cross FS Road 8810
5 2231.5mi, 6:15hr
Emerge onto FS Road 8810, turn R, then cross paved Road 23 (Trout Lake 13.8mi S)
Quartz Creek Butte
3719ft
Riley
South Trail
Swampy Creek
Start
Road 23
Steamboat
Mountain
5376ft
Grand
Meadows Creek
FS Road 88
Mosquito Creek
Steamboat Lake
Trail
Trout Lake Creek
FS Road 8810
FS Road 8851
West Twin
Butte
4716ft
Pataniks
Pushtye
4565ft
East Twin
Butte
4678ft
Eckhart
Point
4592ft
Ninefoot
Peak
4913ft

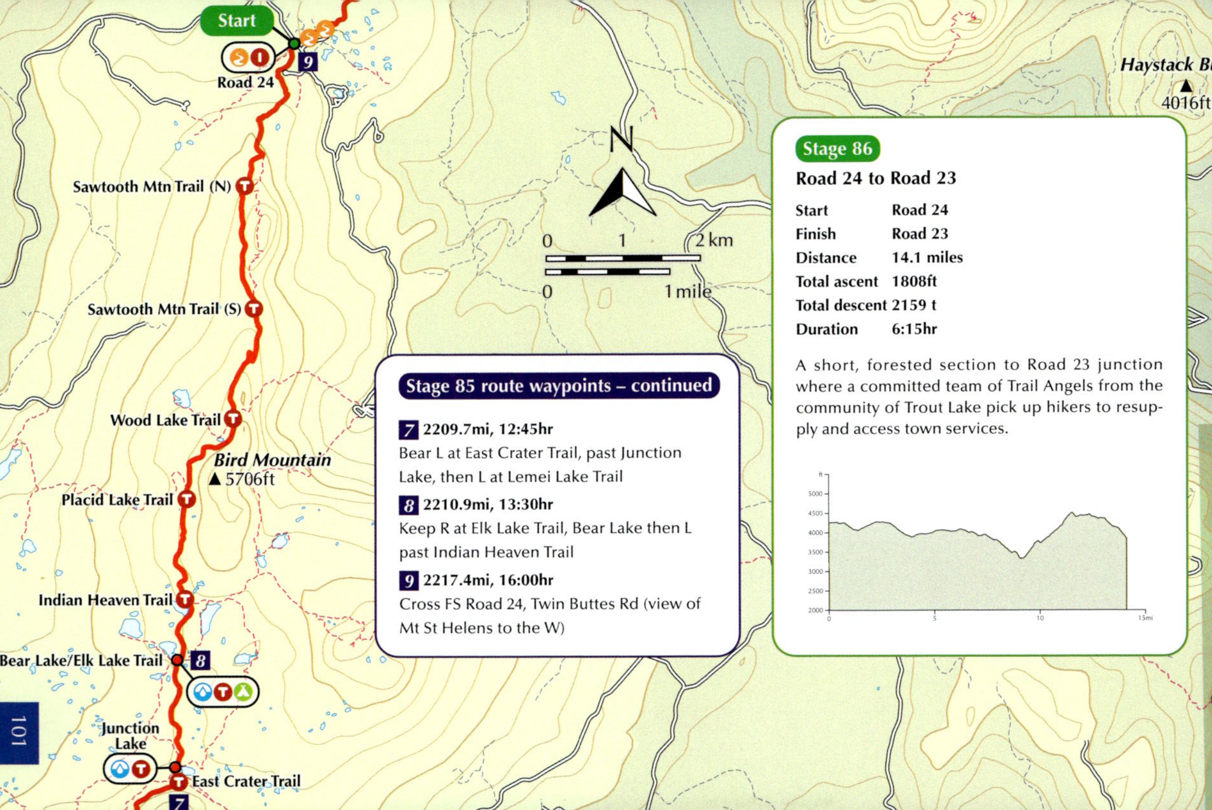

Stage 85 route waypoints – continued

7 2209.7mi, 12:45hr
Bear L at East Crater Trail, past Junction Lake, then L at Lemei Lake Trail

8 2210.9mi, 13:30hr
Keep R at Elk Lake Trail, Bear Lake then L past Indian Heaven Trail

9 2217.4mi, 16:00hr
Cross FS Road 24, Twin Buttes Rd (view of Mt St Helens to the W)

Stage 86

Road 24 to Road 23

Start	**Road 24**
Finish	**Road 23**
Distance	**14.1 miles**
Total ascent	**1808ft**
Total descent	**2159 t**
Duration	**6:15hr**

A short, forested section to Road 23 junction where a committed team of Trail Angels from the community of Trout Lake pick up hikers to resupply and access town services.

Stage 87

Road 23 to Road 5603

Start	**Road 23**
Finish	**Road 5603**
Distance	**22.2 miles**
Total ascent	**3038ft**
Total descent	**2198ft**
Duration	**10:20hr**

An incredibly scenic stage skirting the treeline around Mount Adams with views of the W face and its glaciers. Looking NNW you can see Mount Rainier too. There is plenty of water, but the creeks fed by glaciers will be silty.

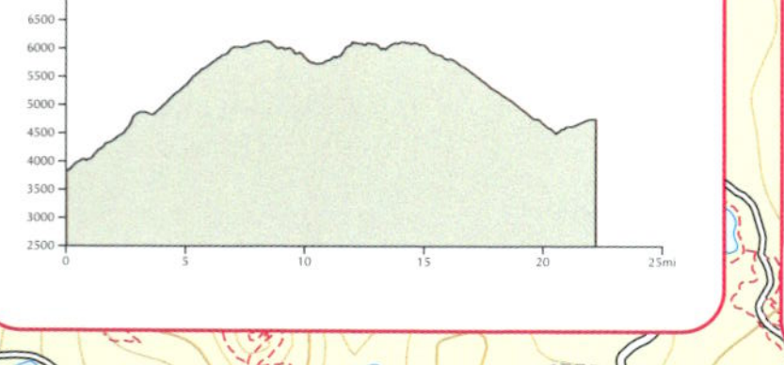

Stage 87 route waypoints

1 2232.5mi, 0:35hr
Shortly after dirt road bridge Swampy Crk, tent sites nearby

2 2238.1mi, 3:45hr
PCT goes L at junction with Round the Mountain Trail, however a short way straight on is seasonal Cascade Crk and tent site

3 2241.7mi, 5:20hr
Pass tent sites by Sheep Lake to cross Riley Crk

4 2246.9mi 7:50hr
Cross Killen Crk on a wooden footbridge

5 2252.1mi, 9:35hr
Shade and excellent water at Lava Spring, tent sites nearby

6 2253.7mi, 10:20hr
Cross FS Road 5603, Potato Hill Trailhead

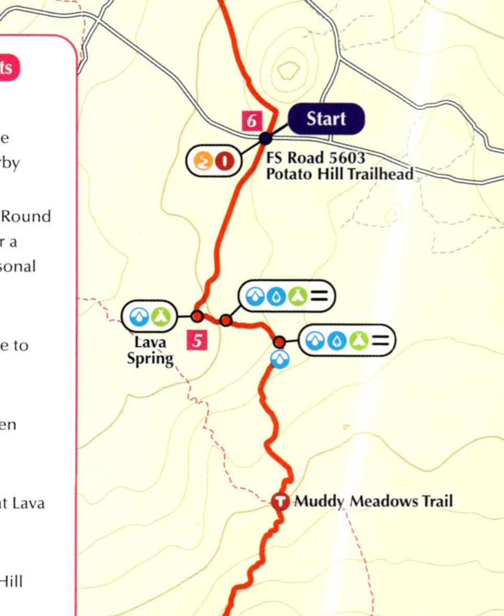

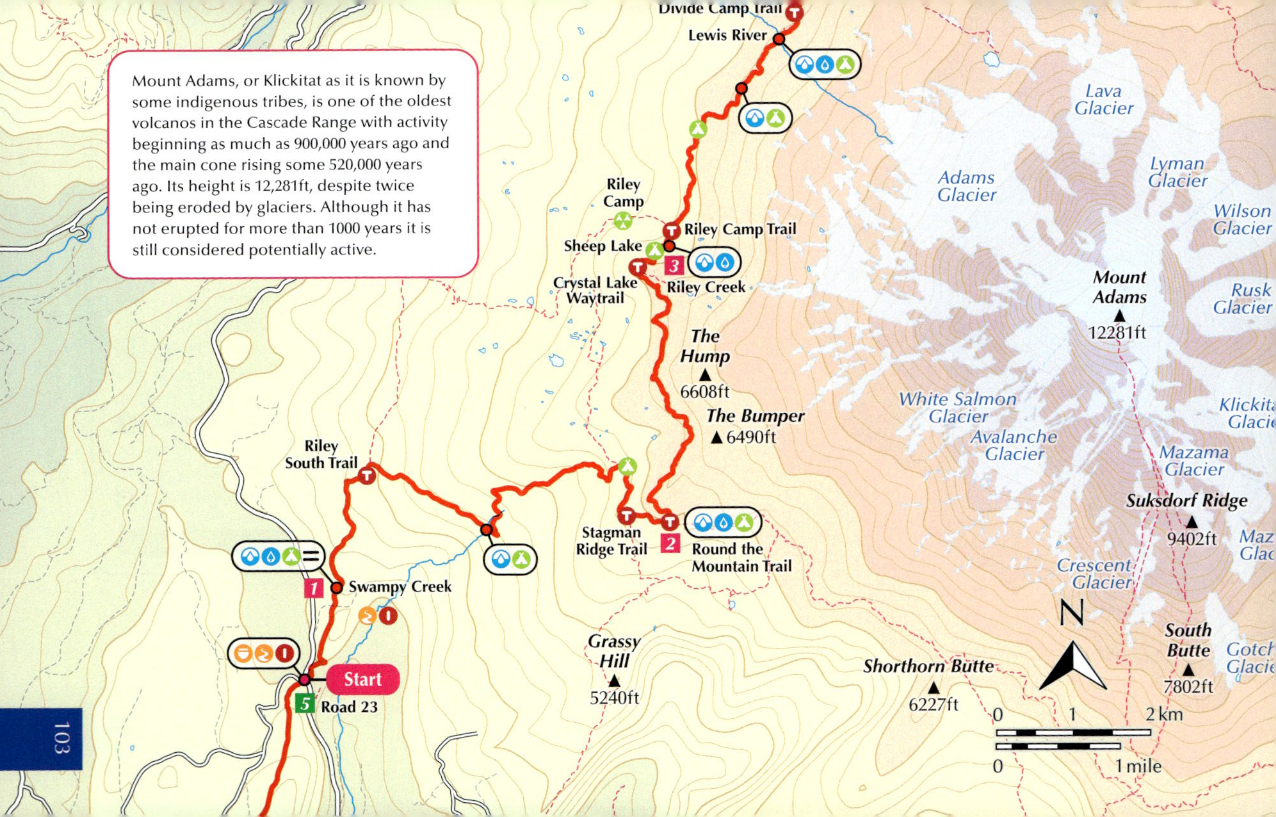
Mount Adams, or Klickitat as it is known by some indigenous tribes, is one of the oldest volcanos in the Cascade Range with activity beginning as much as 900,000 years ago and the main cone rising some 520,000 years ago. Its height is 12,281ft, despite twice being eroded by glaciers. Although it has not erupted for more than 1000 years it is still considered potentially active.
Divide Camp Trail
Lewis River
Riley Camp
Riley Camp Trail
Sheep Lake
3
Riley Creek
Crystal Lake Waytrail
The Hump
6608ft
The Bumper
6490ft
Riley South Trail
Stagman Ridge Trail
2
Round the Mountain Trail
1
Swampy Creek
Start
5
Road 23
Grassy Hill
5240ft
Shorthorn Butte
6227ft
Lava Glacier
Adams Glacier
Lyman Glacier
Wilson Glacier
Mount Adams
12281ft
Rusk Glacier
White Salmon Glacier
Avalanche Glacier
Mazama Glacier
Suksdorf Ridge
9402ft
Crescent Glacier
South Butte
7802ft
N
0
1
2 km
0
1 mile

Stage 88 route waypoints
1 2256.3mi, 0:55hr
Cross Midway Crk, tent sites nearby
2 2260.6mi, 3:00hr
Keep R at Coleman Weedpatch Trail junction on switchback
3 2267.0mi, 5:40hr
Walupt Lake Trail (Walput Lake, campground and trailhead 4mi)
4 2272.0mi, 8:05hr
Bear R past Sheep Lake and Nannie Ridge Trail
5 2274.4mi, 9:20hr
Cross the saddle of Cispus Pass with incredible views
6 2276.6mi, 10:30hr
Keep R past Bypass Trail, 1mi further R past Snowgrass Trail
Keep an eye out and you might see the wild goats that give their name to this wilderness area, and more specifically, to the rugged peaks at the centre of the range, known as Goat Rocks. Protected since 1931, Goat Rocks became part of the National Wilderness Preservation System in 1964. The peaks that remain were once part of a 12,000ft volcano, extinct for some two million years, and eroded to an average of 7000ft, with Gilbert Peak the highest remaining at 8184ft.
North Goat Ridge
6785ft
Packwood Glacier Trail (W)
Old Snowy Mountain
Old Snowy alternate (S)
Peak
7768ft
Ives Peak
7920ft
McCall Glacier
Snowgrass Trail
Big Horn
7999ft
Cispus River
Bypass Trail
6
Conrad Glacier
Meade Glacier
5
Cispus Pass
Cispus River
Nannie Ridge
6138ft
Sheep Lake/ Nannie Ridge Trails
4
Walupt Creek
Nannie Peak
6122ft
Petross Sidehill
5820ft
N
0 1 2 km
0 1 mile

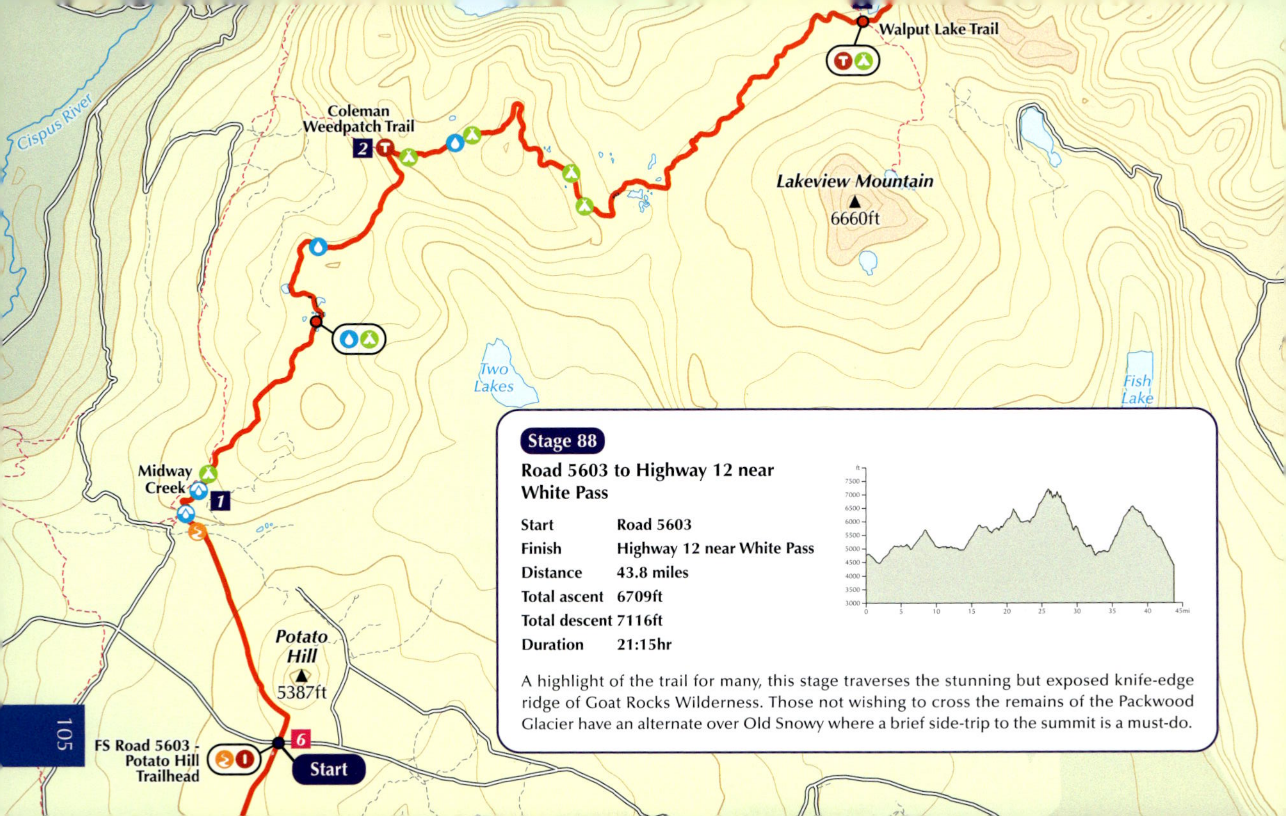

Stage 88

Road 5603 to Highway 12 near White Pass

Start	Road 5603
Finish	Highway 12 near White Pass
Distance	43.8 miles
Total ascent	6709ft
Total descent	7116ft
Duration	21:15hr

A highlight of the trail for many, this stage traverses the stunning but exposed knife-edge ridge of Goat Rocks Wilderness. Those not wishing to cross the remains of the Packwood Glacier have an alternate over Old Snowy where a brief side-trip to the summit is a must-do.

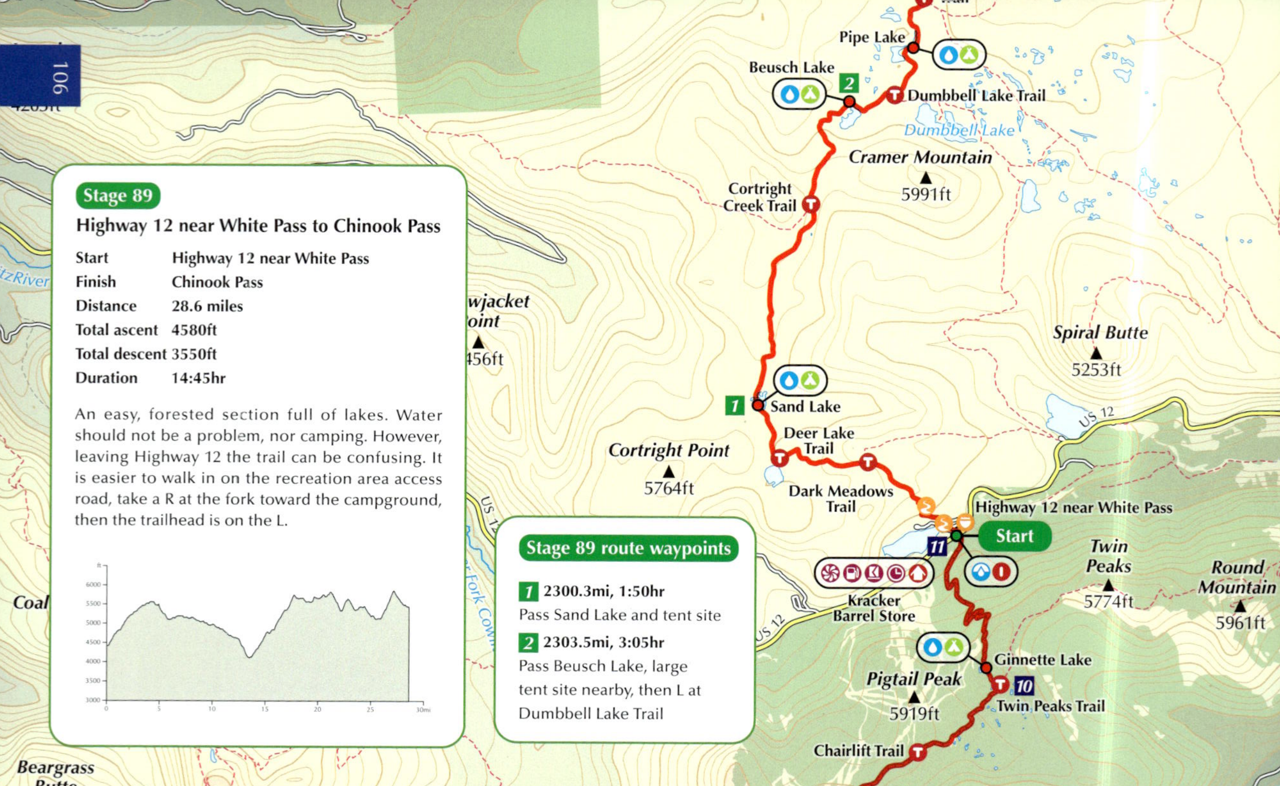

Stage 89

Highway 12 near White Pass to Chinook Pass

Start	Highway 12 near White Pass
Finish	Chinook Pass
Distance	28.6 miles
Total ascent	4580ft
Total descent	3550ft
Duration	14:45hr

An easy, forested section full of lakes. Water should not be a problem, nor camping. However, leaving Highway 12 the trail can be confusing. It is easier to walk in on the recreation area access road, take a R at the fork toward the campground, then the trailhead is on the L.

Stage 89 route waypoints

1 **2300.3mi, 1:50hr**
Pass Sand Lake and tent site

2 **2303.5mi, 3:05hr**
Pass Beusch Lake, large tent site nearby, then L at Dumbbell Lake Trail

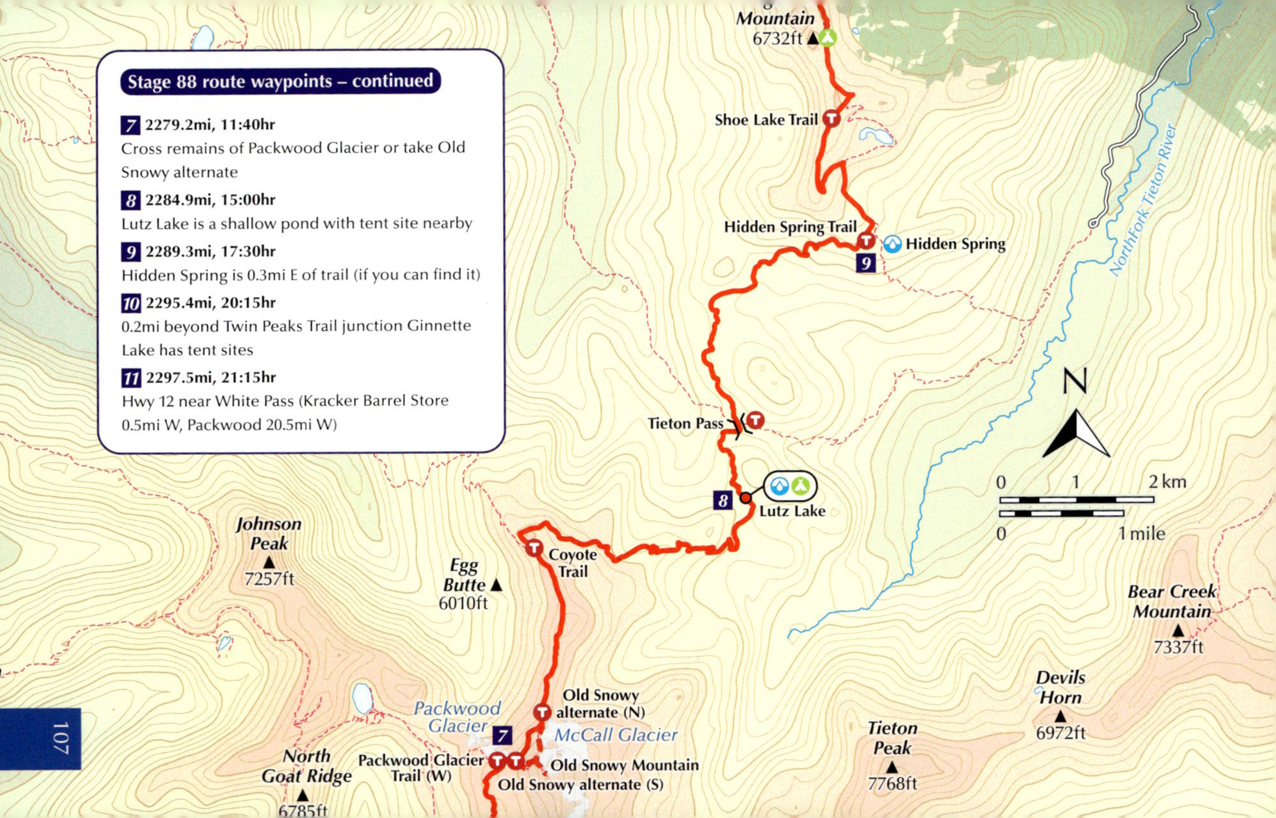

Stage 88 route waypoints – continued
7 2279.2mi, 11:40hr
Cross remains of Packwood Glacier or take Old Snowy alternate
8 2284.9mi, 15:00hr
Lutz Lake is a shallow pond with tent site nearby
9 2289.3mi, 17:30hr
Hidden Spring is 0.3mi E of trail (if you can find it)
10 2295.4mi, 20:15hr
0.2mi beyond Twin Peaks Trail junction Ginnette Lake has tent sites
11 2297.5mi, 21:15hr
Hwy 12 near White Pass (Kracker Barrel Store 0.5mi W, Packwood 20.5mi W)
Mountain
6732ft
Shoe Lake Trail
Hidden Spring Trail
Hidden Spring
9
NorthFork Tieton River
Tieton Pass
8
Lutz Lake
N
0
1
2 km
0
1 mile
Johnson Peak
7257ft
Egg Butte
6010ft
Coyote Trail
Bear Creek Mountain
7337ft
Devils Horn
6972ft
Old Snowy alternate (N)
Packwood Glacier
7
McCall Glacier
Tieton Peak
7768ft
North Goat Ridge
Packwood Glacier Trail (W)
Old Snowy Mountain
Old Snowy alternate (S)

6289ft
Highway 410
Chinook Pass
Chinook Pass
Trailhead
WA
410
9
Start
Tahtlum
Peak
6567ft
N
0
1
2 km
0
1 mile
Naches Peak Loop Trail
WA
123
Buell
Peak
5581ft
Dewey
Lake
8
Dewey Lake Trail
Seymour
Peak
6337ft
Dewey
Peak
6710ft
American River
Anderson
Lake
7
American Lake Trail
Shriner Peak
5833ft
Cougar
Lake
River
Two Lakes Trail
6
Bumping River

Stage 89 route waypoints – continued

3 2305.1mi, 3:40hr
Bear R at fork with Cowlitz Trail

4 2308.3mi, 4:50hr
Keep L past Twin Sisters Trail, then R at Pothole Trail, then bearing N

5 2311.2mi, 6:15hr
Cross Bumping River Ford, turn L at junction with Bumping Lake Trail

6 2317.2mi, 10:00hr
Keep L at Two Lakes Trail, several tent sites nearby

7 2319.8mi, 11:10hr
Keep L past American Lake Trail junction

8 2323.0mi, 12:30hr
Reach Dewey Lake, several potential tent sites

9 2326.1mi, 14:45hr
Bridge over Hwy 410, Chinook Pass

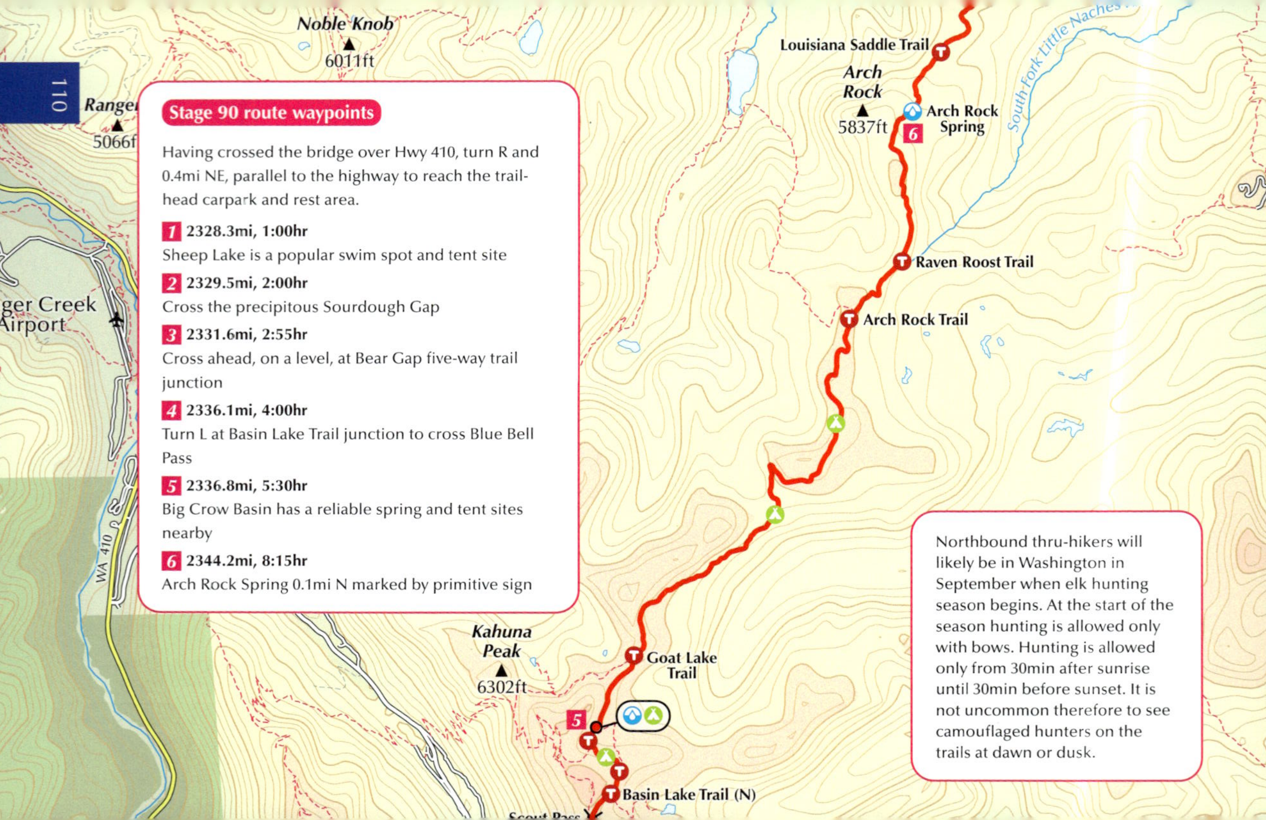

Stage 90 route waypoints

Having crossed the bridge over Hwy 410, turn R and 0.4mi NE, parallel to the highway to reach the trail-head carpark and rest area.

1 2328.3mi, 1:00hr
Sheep Lake is a popular swim spot and tent site

2 2329.5mi, 2:00hr
Cross the precipitous Sourdough Gap

3 2331.6mi, 2:55hr
Cross ahead, on a level, at Bear Gap five-way trail junction

4 2336.1mi, 4:00hr
Turn L at Basin Lake Trail junction to cross Blue Bell Pass

5 2336.8mi, 5:30hr
Big Crow Basin has a reliable spring and tent sites nearby

6 2344.2mi, 8:15hr
Arch Rock Spring 0.1mi N marked by primitive sign

Northbound thru-hikers will likely be in Washington in September when elk hunting season begins. At the start of the season hunting is allowed only with bows. Hunting is allowed only from 30min after sunrise until 30min before sunset. It is not uncommon therefore to see camouflaged hunters on the trails at dawn or dusk.

Stage 90

Chinook Pass to Road 784

Start	Chinook Pass
Finish	Road 784
Distance	32 miles
Total ascent	4327ft
Total descent	4833ft
Duration	13:50hr

An airy series of ridges and passes means limited water. This stage has also seen significant fire damage so expect long stretches with little shade. Big Crow Spring and Arch Rock Spring are small but important sources of water in an otherwise dry stretch.

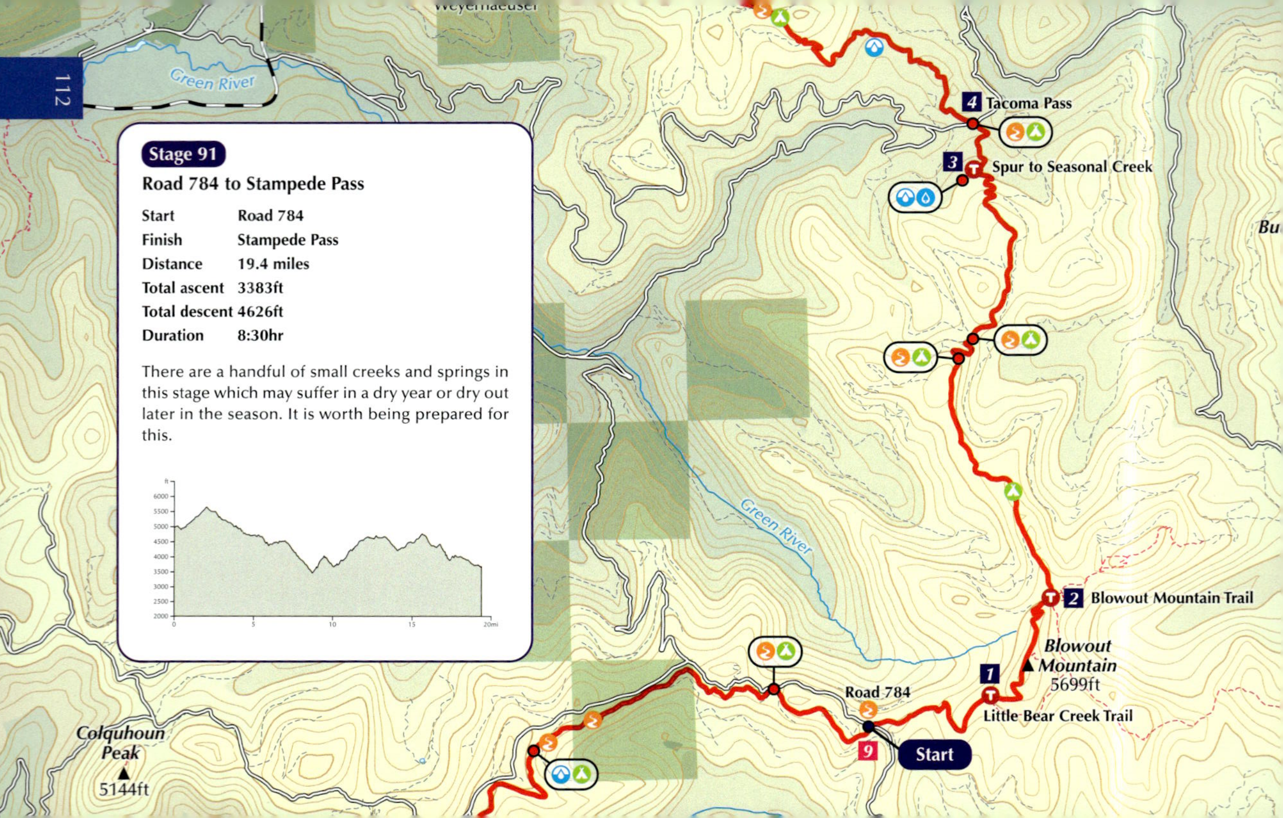

Stage 91

Road 784 to Stampede Pass

Start	Road 784
Finish	Stampede Pass
Distance	19.4 miles
Total ascent	3383ft
Total descent	4626ft
Duration	8:30hr

There are a handful of small creeks and springs in this stage which may suffer in a dry year or dry out later in the season. It is worth being prepared for this.

Stage 91 route waypoints

1 2359.5mi, 0:45hr
Little Bear Creek Trail drops E of Blowout Mountain crossing reliable Blowout Crk then climbing N to rejoin PCT at:

2 2361.0mi, 1:30hr
Blowout Mountain Trail junction

3 2366.1mi, 3:25hr
Spur trail to seasonal creek 0.1mi SW

4 2366.7mi, 3:35hr
Cross FS Road 52, Tacoma Pass

Stage 90 route waypoints - continued

7 2349.6mi, 10:15hr
Camp Ulrich cabin (emergency use), creek and outhouse

8 2351.3mi, 11:25hr
Windy Gap, end of dirt road, tent site

9 2358.1mi, 13:50hr
Cross Road 784

Stage 92 route waypoints

1 2382.4mi, 1:55hr
Cross Stirrup Lake Trail, then Stirrup Crk

2 2386.0mi, 3:20hr
Cross Yakima Pass with the small Twilight Lake nearby

3 2386.5mi, 4:20hr
Cross Mirror Lake outlet twice, several tent sites beside lake, pass Mirror Lake Trail on R far end of lake

4 2391.0mi, 6:15hr
Cross Olallie Crk at N end of Olallie Meadow

5 2391.7mi, 6:35hr
Join FS Road 110, turn R for 0.2mi, then turn L downhill

Stage 91 route waypoints – continued

5 2373.2mi, 6:40hr
Small spring 50ft downhill off trail

6 2377.5mi, 8:30hr
Stampede Pass (Lizard Lake is a short walk SW if water is needed)

Stage 92

Stampede Pass to Interstate 90 Snoqualmie Pass

Start	Stampede Pass
Finish	Interstate 90 Snoqualmie Pass
Distance	18.3 miles
Total ascent	3268ft
Total descent	3973ft
Duration	8:20hr

Clear-cut logging is evident throughout this stage, which suffered under private ownership for many years before being purchased by the Forest Service. There are usually sufficient water sources, however.

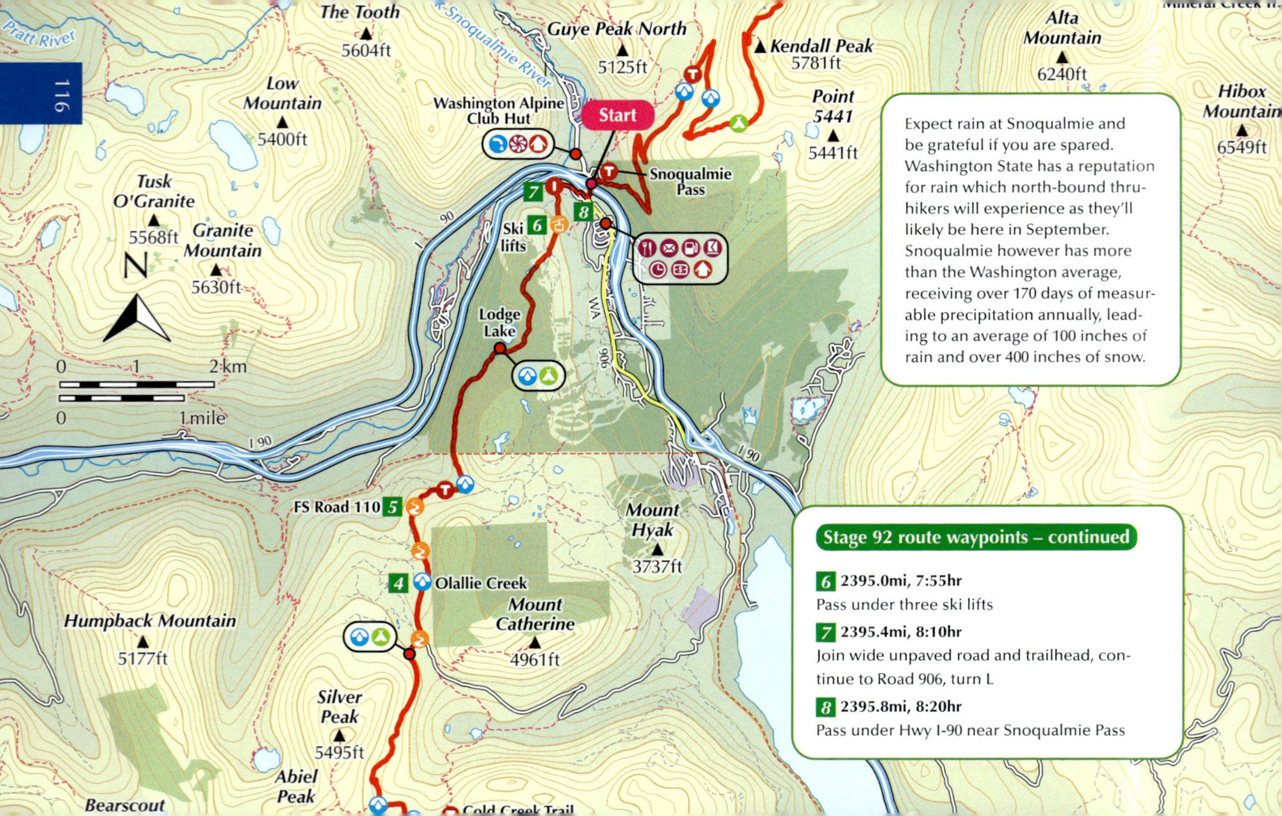

Expect rain at Snoqualmie and be grateful if you are spared. Washington State has a reputation for rain which north-bound thru-hikers will experience as they'll likely be here in September. Snoqualmie however has more than the Washington average, receiving over 170 days of measurable precipitation annually, leading to an average of 100 inches of rain and over 400 inches of snow.

Stage 92 route waypoints – continued

6 2395.0mi, 7:55hr
Pass under three ski lifts

7 2395.4mi, 8:10hr
Join wide unpaved road and trailhead, continue to Road 906, turn L

8 2395.8mi, 8:20hr
Pass under Hwy I-90 near Snoqualmie Pass

SECTION 11 – INTERSTATE 90 SNOQUALMIE PASS TO NORTHERN TERMINUS

	Stage	Distance (miles)	Total ascent (feet)	Total descent (feet)	Average duration (hr:min)	Page
93	I-90 Snoqualmie Pass – Waptus River	34.7	7549	7467	18:55	122
94	Waptus River – Stevens Pass	36.2	7474	6476	19:40	125
95	Stevens Pass – Indian Pass	34.2	7041	6148	17:00	126
96	Indian Pass – Suiattle River	42.3	8107	10,696	19:50	131
97	Suiattle River – Stehekin River	31.3	5000	5850	13:20	132
98	Stehekin River – Rainy Pass	19.3	4580	1325	9:20	135
99	Rainy Pass – Hart's Pass	30.9	5922	4577	14:50	137
100	Hart's Pass – Northern Terminus	30.5	4485	6424	14:30	139
Totals		**259.4**	**50,158**	**48,963**	**127:25**	

WHAT TO EXPECT

North of Snoqualmie Pass the trail leads into rugged country, some of the most challenging and remote terrain since the Sierra Nevada. Climbing quickly to the crest of the Cascade Range, the PCT crosses the notorious Kendall Katwalk, a quite exposed 150-yard long path blasted out across a steeply sloped granite face on the north ridge of Kendall Peak. The tall peaks and deep valleys of the Alpine Lakes Wilderness are the product of uplift and faulting followed by the last glacial retreat between 10–14,000 years ago which left the distinctive U-shaped river valleys of Lemah Creek and the Waptus River.

In Glacier Peak Wilderness, beyond Steven's Pass, the trail traverses the precipitous west and north-facing slopes of the 10,541ft Glacier Peak, named for the greatest concentration of active glaciers in the lower 48 states. The North Cascades accumulate more snow than anywhere else in the US. The slopes are avalanche prone, and from year-to-year trail conditions can vary enormously. Trail maintenance here is slow, the season is short, and the work must all be carried out by hand, without mechanized assistance due to the wilderness designation. If bridges are out on the White Chuck or Suiattle Rivers in particular, the crossings would be quite dangerous. Protected since 1960 the wilderness is home to a rich variety of wildlife including elk, deer, cougar, black bear, mountain goat, marten and lynx.

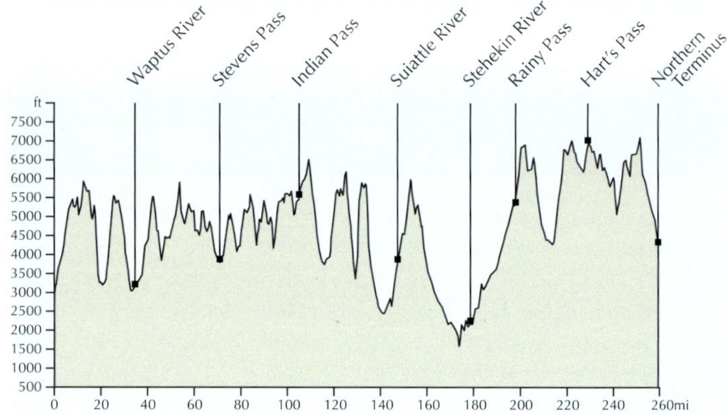

Bear-proof food canisters are recommended here, where bears are common, especially between the Suiattle River and Stehekin River. Few hikers will pass the opportunity to visit Stehekin, a remote community at the head of the 50-mile long Lake Chelan. The name originates from the Salishan language and means 'the way through', appropriate for hikers bridging the river before climbing out to the aptly named Rainy Pass.

North of Rainy Pass the only road access is a gravel track that climbs from the community of Mazama to Hart's Pass, thanks to the region's history of mining. Beyond, the Pasayten Wilderness offers spectacular views, especially in late September when larch, spruce and maple trees deliver their fall display. The terrain here is a mix of wooded valleys and high meadows, where the trail climbs a succession of rugged ridges before the final wooded descent to an unassuming firebreak in the trees, where a wooden monument, not unlike one on the southern US border, awaits.

August and September provide the short window of opportunity for hiking in this northern section. In a low-snow year southbound thru-hikers might start in mid July, but local information on conditions is necessary to be confident of safe passage. Storms begin rolling in through September, and around early October the first snows arrive, quickly covering this wonderland for another year.

Resupply options are quite limited. Packages sent to Stevens Pass and Stehekin are the best way to restock. A hitch from Stevens to Skykomish is possible if store access is necessary. Otherwise, a tough hitch from Hart's Pass to Mazama will reward the patient hiker.

PEN
Princeton
Hope
Manning
Park
CANADA
ABBOTSFORD
PCT Northern
Terminus
USA
100
N
Mazama
99
98
0
25
50
km
0
25 miles
Stehekin
97
Lake Chelan
96
Skykomish
95
Leavenworth
SEATTLE
93
North Bend
Interstate 90
94
WENATCHEE
TACOMA
Cle Elum

RESUPPLY OPTIONS

Stage	Trail mile	Place	Off trail (miles)	Description	Facilities
94	2466.7	Stevens Pass	On trail	Ski Resort, accepts packages has café and restaurant	
94	2466.7	Stevens Pass	0.3 W	Mountaineers Lodge (accepts PCT hikers as temp members)	
94	2466.7	Skykomish	16.0 W	Small community with gas station mini-mart, library, PO and diner	
97	2574.5	Stehekin	11.0 SE	Remote community, camping, lodge w/small store and restaurant	
98	2593.8	Mazama	22.4 E	Small community, cabins, store, inn and outfitter accepts packages	

PERMITS

Permits are required in Alpine Lakes Wilderness, PCT miles 2397.3 to 2463.2, North Cascades National Park, PCT miles 2572.5 to 2590.4 and Pasayten Wilderness, PCT miles 2629.9 to 2655.2.

Alpine Lakes Wilderness/Pasayten Wilderness

Wilderness permits are required for day use and overnight use in all Okanogan-Wenatchee Wildernesses. The self-issued permits are free and are available at all trailheads leading into these Wildernesses, and at Forest Service Ranger Stations.

For more information call the Naches Ranger District office at (509) 653-1401 or visit: www.fs.usda.gov/detail/okawen/passes-permits/?cid=fsbdev3_053610#norse%20peak

North Cascades National Park

Wilderness permits are required for overnight use. Camping is only allowed at designated sites (no dispersed camping), and permits are limited to the number of sites and site capacity of each backcountry camp. NOTE: Many hikers pass through the 18 miles of the PCT within the park without spending the night. If hikers are not spending the night at any camp, a park permit is not needed.

Two thirds of the available quota are made available in advance for

Traversing the ridge below Hogback Mountain (Stage 93)

reservation with a lottery operating for early access in March, the remainder becoming available for reservation in April. The remaining one third are available on a walk-up basis up to one day before your trip from Wilderness Information Centers.

To obtain a permit visit: www.recreation.gov/permits/4675322

For more information contact the Wilderness Information Center at noca_wilderness@nps.gov for assistance or visit: www.nps.gov/noca/planyourvisit/permits.htm

MAIL DROP INFORMATION

Stevens Pass
'Your Name Here and ETA'
c/o Stevens Pass, Through Hiker
93001 NE Stevens Pass Hwy, US 2
Skykomish, WA 98288
They are open: Mon–Sun 9am–6pm
Phone them on: (206) 812-4510
Visit them at: www.stevenspass.com

Mazama
'Your Name Here and ETA'
c/o Goats Beard Mountain Supply
44 Lost River Road
Mazama, WA 98833
They are open: Mon–Sun 9am–5pm
Phone them on: (509) 996-2515
Visit them at: https://goatsbeardmountainsupplies.com

POST OFFICE INFORMATION

'Your Name Here'
c\o General Delivery
Skykomish, WA 98288
ETA: 'Your ETA'
Located at: 108 Thelma Street
Phone them on: (360) 677-2241

'Your Name Here'
c/o General Delivery
Stehekin, WA 98852
ETA: 'Your ETA'
Located at: 31 Defacto Lane
Phone them on:
(509) 699-2015

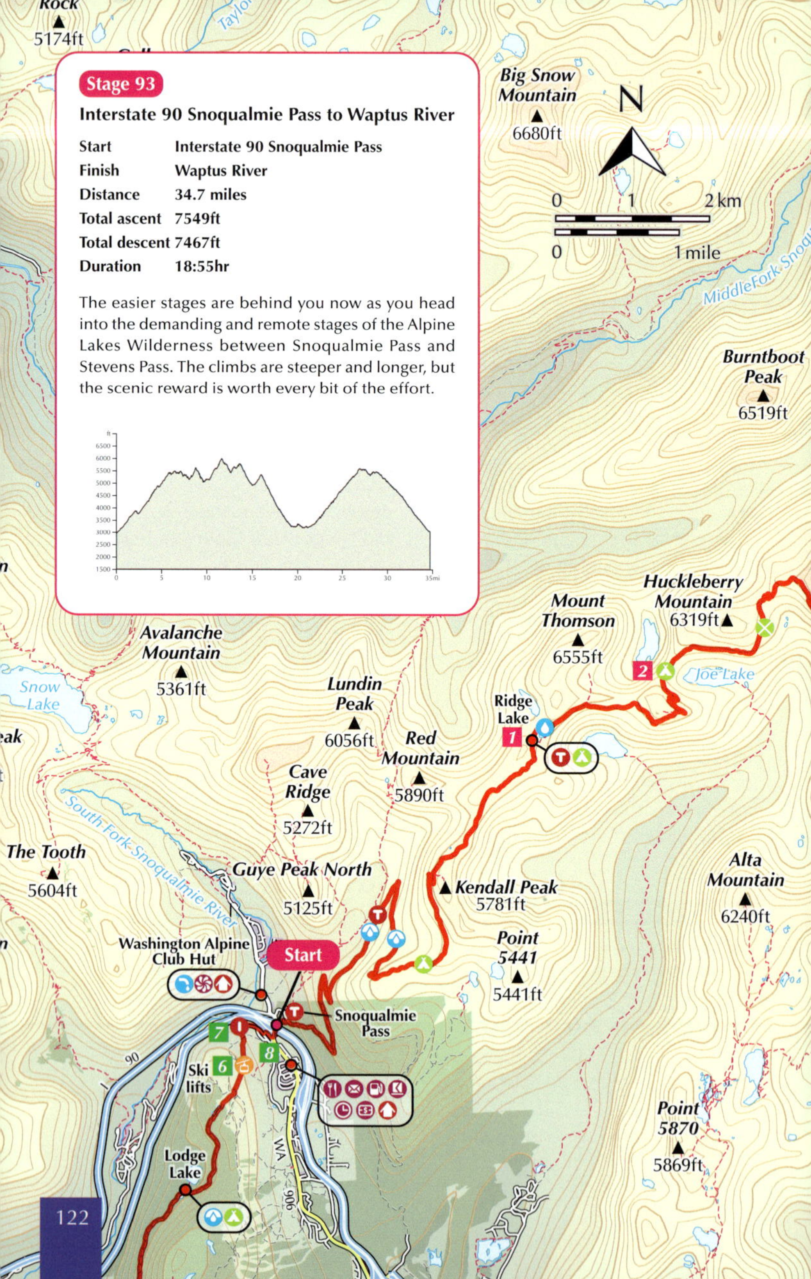

Stage 93
Interstate 90 Snoqualmie Pass to Waptus River
Start Interstate 90 Snoqualmie Pass
Finish Waptus River
Distance 34.7 miles
Total ascent 7549ft
Total descent 7467ft
Duration 18:55hr
The easier stages are behind you now as you head into the demanding and remote stages of the Alpine Lakes Wilderness between Snoqualmie Pass and Stevens Pass. The climbs are steeper and longer, but the scenic reward is worth every bit of the effort.
ft
6500
6000
5500
5000
4500
4000
3500
3000
2500
2000
1500
0
5
10
15
20
25
30
35mi
Rock
5174ft
Taylor
Big Snow Mountain
6680ft
N
0
1
2 km
0
1 mile
Middle Fork Snoq
Burntboot Peak
6519ft
Huckleberry Mountain
6319ft
Mount Thomson
6555ft
Joe Lake
2
Ridge Lake
1
Avalanche Mountain
5361ft
Snow Lake
Lundin Peak
6056ft
Red Mountain
5890ft
Cave Ridge
5272ft
South Fork Snoqualmie River
The Tooth
5604ft
Guye Peak North
5125ft
Kendall Peak
5781ft
Alta Mountain
6240ft
Point 5441
5441ft
Washington Alpine Club Hut
Start
Snoqualmie Pass
7
8
6
Ski lifts
90
WA
906
Lodge Lake
Point 5870
5869ft

Bears Breast Mountain
7198ft
Spade Lake
7124
Vicente Point
6640ft
Waptus River
Middle Chief Peak
7119ft
Overcoat Glacier
Overcoat Peak
7431ft
Overcoat Glacier
Waptus River
Start
Spade Creek
Dutch Miller Gap Trail
7
Waptus River Trail
Spade Lake Trail
Escondido Point
6178ft
Cooper River
6
Waptus Lake
Chimney Glacier
Waptus Burn Trail
Lemah Mountain
7480ft
Lemah Meadow Trail
Tributary of Lemah Creek
Chikamin Peak
6923ft
Lemah Creek
5
Pete Lake
Pete Lake Trail
Island Mountain
4475ft
Four Brothers
6486ft
Spectacle Lake
4
Delate Creek
Spectacle Lake Trail
3
Mineral Creek Trail
Three Queens
6686ft
East Chikamin Point
5620ft
Hibox Mountain
6549ft
Ridge
Stage 93 route waypoints
1 2402.9mi, 5:10hr
Tent site before Ridge Lake, (small use trail circles lake)
2 2405.0mi, 6:05hr
Tent sites either end of saddle between Edds Lake and Joe Lake
3 2410.0mi, 8:30hr
Trail to stock camp, spring-fed pools, and then Mineral Creek Trail
4 2413.8mi, 10:20hr
Cross Delate Crk on bridge, tent sites nearby
5 2416.4mi, 11:30hr
Cross Lemah Crk (bridge washed out), tributary ahead has bridge
6 2423.8mi, 14:50hr
Cross headwaters of Cooper River near small lake
7 2430.5mi, 18:55hr
Bridge over Waptus River (0.1mi E to large tent site)
The Alpine Lakes Wilderness features some of the most rugged topography in the Cascade Range, with craggy peaks and ridges, deep glacial valleys, and granite walls, as well as hosting over 700 mountain lakes.

Stage 94 route waypoints

1 2437.4mi, 3:50hr
Turn R at Deep Lake Trail to remain on PCT

2 2440.4mi, 5:50hr
Turn R at Circle Lake Trail, top Cathedral Pass, ignore ridge trail, then keep L past Cathedral Pass Trail

3 2445.5mi, 8:25hr
Deception Pass, three trails intersect, L at first, then keep R at next two

4 2450.8mi, 11:30hr
Cross the scenic Pieper Pass

5 2453.2mi, 13:10hr
Turn R at Surprise Creek Trail

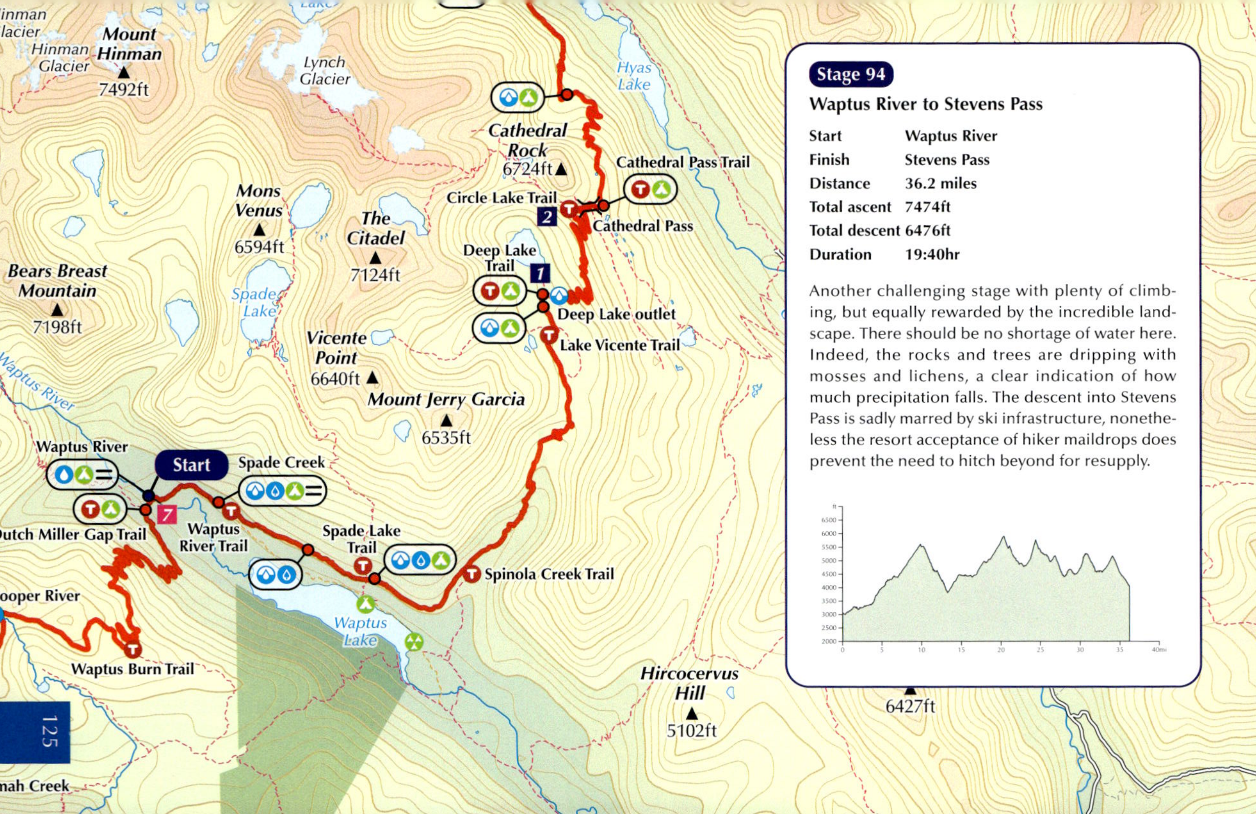

Stage 94

Waptus River to Stevens Pass

Start	Waptus River
Finish	Stevens Pass
Distance	36.2 miles
Total ascent	7474ft
Total descent	6476ft
Duration	19:40hr

Another challenging stage with plenty of climbing, but equally rewarded by the incredible landscape. There should be no shortage of water here. Indeed, the rocks and trees are dripping with mosses and lichens, a clear indication of how much precipitation falls. The descent into Stevens Pass is sadly marred by ski infrastructure, nonetheless the resort acceptance of hiker maildrops does prevent the need to hitch beyond for resupply.

Stage 95

Stevens Pass to Indian Pass

Start	Stevens Pass
Finish	Indian Pass
Distance	34.2 miles
Total ascent	7041ft
Total descent	6148 t
Duration	17:00hr

Now deep into the North Cascades the trail is becoming tougher, avalanche damage is more common, and bridges may be damaged or washed out. In places the trail can hold snow all year too, so you may start to encounter snow again even if you haven't seen any for a while. You'll also need to take greater precautions with food as bears are much greater in number here than anywhere further south.

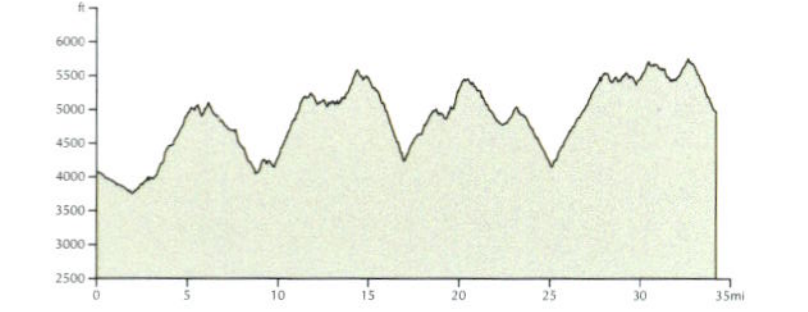

Stage 94 route waypoints – continued
6 2458.5mi, 15:40hr
Keep R at Tunnel Creek Trail, past Hope Lake, then Mig Lake
7 2462.5mi, 17:40hr
Lake Susan Jane has a campground and toilets
8 2466.7mi, 19:40hr
Descend to Hwy 2 at Stevens Pass (Mountaineers Lodge 0.3mi W, Skykomish 16mi W)
Lake
Tunnel Creek Trail
Trap Lake Trail
Trap Pass Trail
Surprise Creek Trail
Nimbus Mountain
6713ft
Spark Plug Mountain
6276ft
Glacier Lake
Glacier Lake inlet
6555ft
Pieper Pass
Surprise Gap Trail
Square Lake
Surprise Mountain Trail
Deception Lake outlet
Deception Creek Trail (N)
Mac Peak
6818ft
Sawyer
5502ft
Terrace Mountain
6362ft
N
0
1
2 km
1 mile

Stage 95 route waypoints

The trail out of Stevens Pass isn't obvious. Take bridge over highway to large parking area, bear R to northernmost corner, trail commences past an electricity substation.

1 2470.3mi, 1:20hr
Several tent sites close to water at Nason Crk

2 2476.5mi, 4:30hr
Side trail to lake camp area at Lake Janus

3 2481.2mi, 7:25hr
Small tent site on Grizzly Peak, one either side also

4 2485.2mi, 9:30hr
Take R fork at Meadow Creek Trail (good tent sites 0.1mi L to Pear Lake)

5 2490.3mi, 11:50hr
West Cady Ridge Trail (8mi W to trailhead)

6 2491.8mi, 12:20hr
Descend to Pass Creek Trail (L), then climb 0.4mi to Cady Creek Trail (R)

7 2496.1mi, 14:50hr
Lake Sally Ann sits in a stunning cirque

8 2497.7mi, 15:30hr
Keep R at unmarked North Fork Skykomish/Bald Eagle Trail junction

9 2500.9mi, 17:00hr
Keep L at Indian Pass junction with Indian Creek Trail

Fall Mountain
5568ft
Shoofly Mountain
5404ft
5840ft
Fortune Mountain
5879ft
4
Meadow Creek Trail
Top Lake Trail
Wenatchee Pass
Heather Lake
Labyrinth Mountain
6257ft
Grizzly Peak
5463ft
3
Grizzly Peak
Scrabble Mountain
5692ft
Lake Janus
2
Jove Peak
5925ft
Union Peak
5696ft
Smithbrook Trail
N
0
1
2 km
0
1 mile

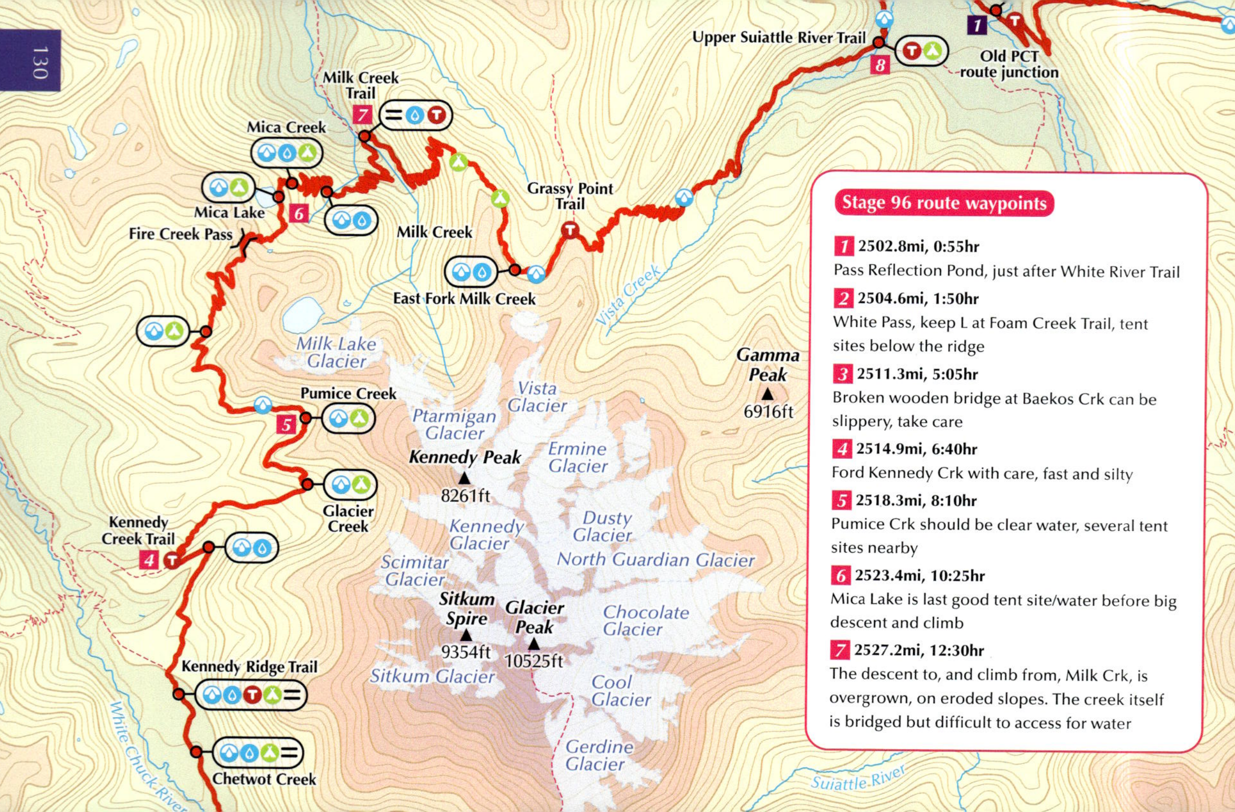

Stage 96 route waypoints
1 2502.8mi, 0:55hr
Pass Reflection Pond, just after White River Trail
2 2504.6mi, 1:50hr
White Pass, keep L at Foam Creek Trail, tent sites below the ridge
3 2511.3mi, 5:05hr
Broken wooden bridge at Baekos Crk can be slippery, take care
4 2514.9mi, 6:40hr
Ford Kennedy Crk with care, fast and silty
5 2518.3mi, 8:10hr
Pumice Crk should be clear water, several tent sites nearby
6 2523.4mi, 10:25hr
Mica Lake is last good tent site/water before big descent and climb
7 2527.2mi, 12:30hr
The descent to, and climb from, Milk Crk, is overgrown, on eroded slopes. The creek itself is bridged but difficult to access for water
Upper Suiattle River Trail
Old PCT route junction
Milk Creek Trail
Mica Creek
Mica Lake
Fire Creek Pass
Milk Creek
Grassy Point Trail
East Fork Milk Creek
Vista Creek
Milk Lake Glacier
Pumice Creek
Ptarmigan Glacier
Vista Glacier
Gamma Peak
6916ft
Kennedy Peak
8261ft
Ermine Glacier
Glacier Creek
Kennedy Creek Trail
Kennedy Glacier
Dusty Glacier
North Guardian Glacier
Scimitar Glacier
Sitkum Spire
9354ft
Glacier Peak
10525ft
Chocolate Glacier
Sitkum Glacier
Cool Glacier
Kennedy Ridge Trail
Chetwot Creek
Gerdine Glacier
White Chuck River
Suiattle River

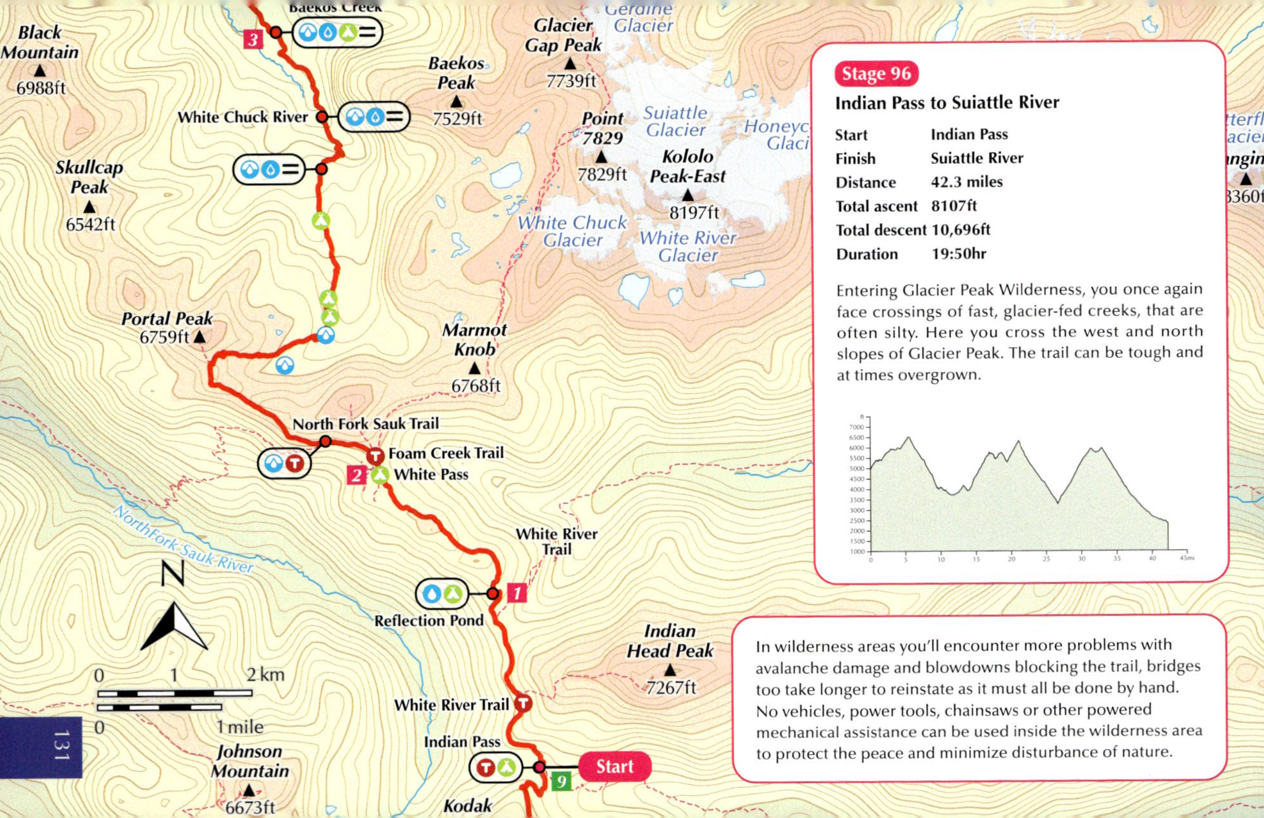

Stage 96

Indian Pass to Suiattle River

Start	Indian Pass
Finish	Suiattle River
Distance	42.3 miles
Total ascent	8107ft
Total descent	10,696ft
Duration	19:50hr

Entering Glacier Peak Wilderness, you once again face crossings of fast, glacier-fed creeks, that are often silty. Here you cross the west and north slopes of Glacier Peak. The trail can be tough and at times overgrown.

In wilderness areas you'll encounter more problems with avalanche damage and blowdowns blocking the trail, bridges too take longer to reinstate as it must all be done by hand. No vehicles, power tools, chainsaws or other powered mechanical assistance can be used inside the wilderness area to protect the peace and minimize disturbance of nature.

Stage 97

Suiattle River to Stehekin River

Start	**Suiattle River**
Finish	**Stehekin River**
Distance	**31.3 miles**
Total ascent	**5000ft**
Total descent	**5850ft**
Duration	**13:20hr**

Despite the initial 3000ft climb to Suiattle Pass, this is a relatively easy stage with a long gentle descent. Just 0.3 miles before you reach the Stehekin River you enter the North Cascades National Park and camping is limited to designated sites, just Bridge Creek Camp and Six Mile Camp can be used without an additional permit. Most will take the bus to resupply at Stehekin, with its Post Office, perhaps the smallest on the whole PCT. If you need to exit the trail here a regular ferry traverses the 50 miles of lake to the community of Chelan.

There is probably the highest density of bears here of any area you have passed through. In 2023 a horse died near High Bridge and the carcass attracted so many bears that the area had to be closed temporarily. Bears had even been bold enough to cross the bridge, at the same time as hikers!

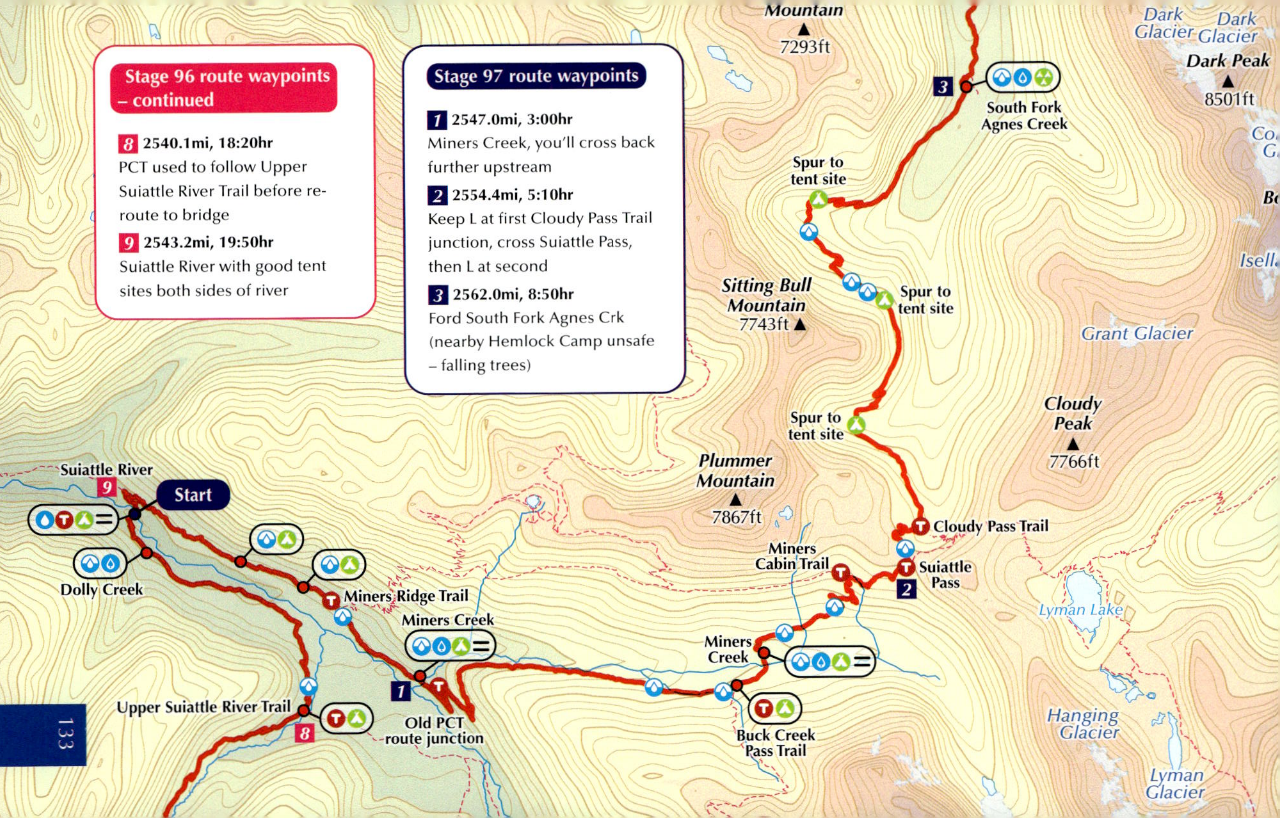

Stage 96 route waypoints – continued

8 2540.1mi, 18:20hr
PCT used to follow Upper Suiattle River Trail before re-route to bridge

9 2543.2mi, 19:50hr
Suiattle River with good tent sites both sides of river

Stage 97 route waypoints

1 2547.0mi, 3:00hr
Miners Creek, you'll cross back further upstream

2 2554.4mi, 5:10hr
Keep L at first Cloudy Pass Trail junction, cross Suiattle Pass, then L at second

3 2562.0mi, 8:50hr
Ford South Fork Agnes Crk (nearby Hemlock Camp unsafe – falling trees)

Stage 98

Stehekin River to Rainy Pass

Start	Stehekin River
Finish	Rainy Pass
Distance	19.3 miles
Total ascent	4580ft
Total descent	1325ft
Duration	9:20hr

This shorter stage climbs gently alongside first Stehekin River, and then Bridge Creek all the way to Rainy Pass. It is a popular hiking area despite its relative remoteness.

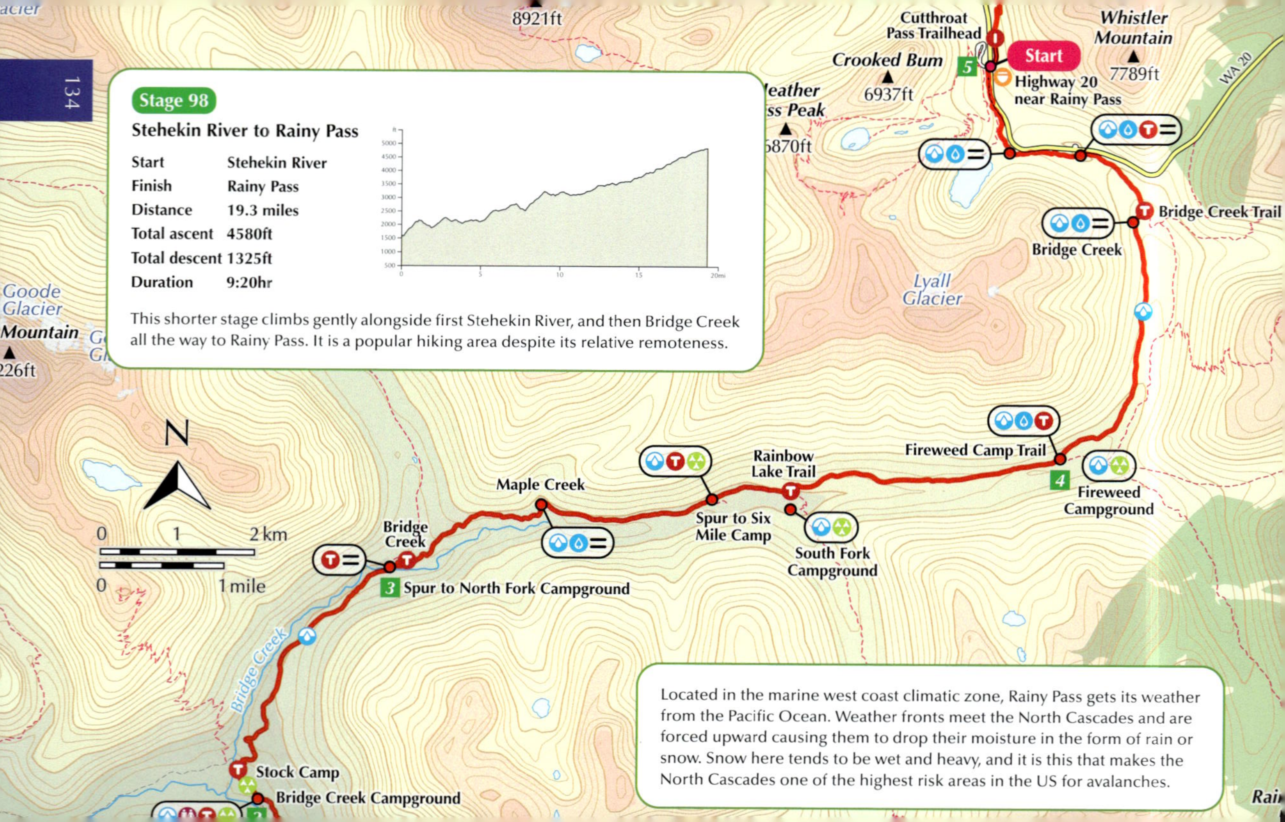

Located in the marine west coast climatic zone, Rainy Pass gets its weather from the Pacific Ocean. Weather fronts meet the North Cascades and are forced upward causing them to drop their moisture in the form of rain or snow. Snow here tends to be wet and heavy, and it is this that makes the North Cascades one of the highest risk areas in the US for avalanches.

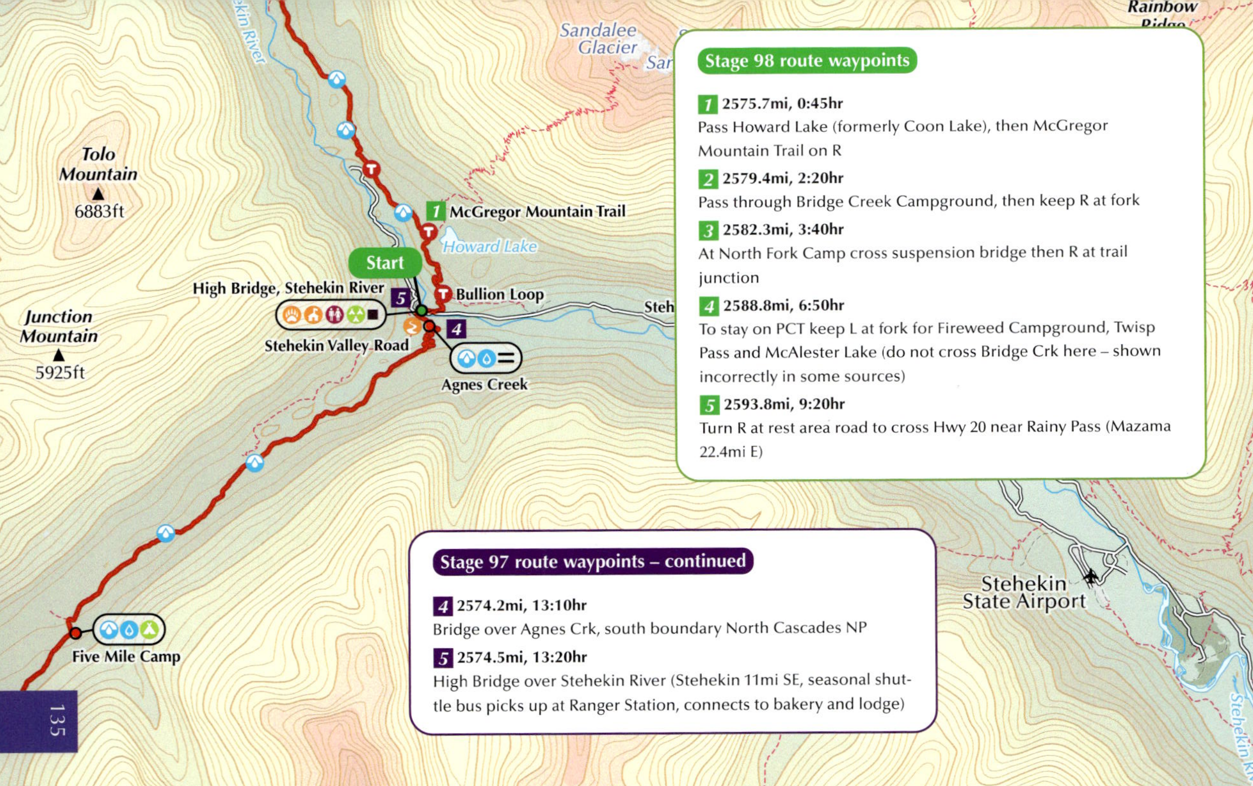

Stage 98 route waypoints

1 2575.7mi, 0:45hr
Pass Howard Lake (formerly Coon Lake), then McGregor Mountain Trail on R

2 2579.4mi, 2:20hr
Pass through Bridge Creek Campground, then keep R at fork

3 2582.3mi, 3:40hr
At North Fork Camp cross suspension bridge then R at trail junction

4 2588.8mi, 6:50hr
To stay on PCT keep L at fork for Fireweed Campground, Twisp Pass and McAlester Lake (do not cross Bridge Crk here – shown incorrectly in some sources)

5 2593.8mi, 9:20hr
Turn R at rest area road to cross Hwy 20 near Rainy Pass (Mazama 22.4mi E)

Stage 97 route waypoints – continued

4 2574.2mi, 13:10hr
Bridge over Agnes Crk, south boundary North Cascades NP

5 2574.5mi, 13:20hr
High Bridge over Stehekin River (Stehekin 11mi SE, seasonal shuttle bus picks up at Ranger Station, connects to bakery and lodge)

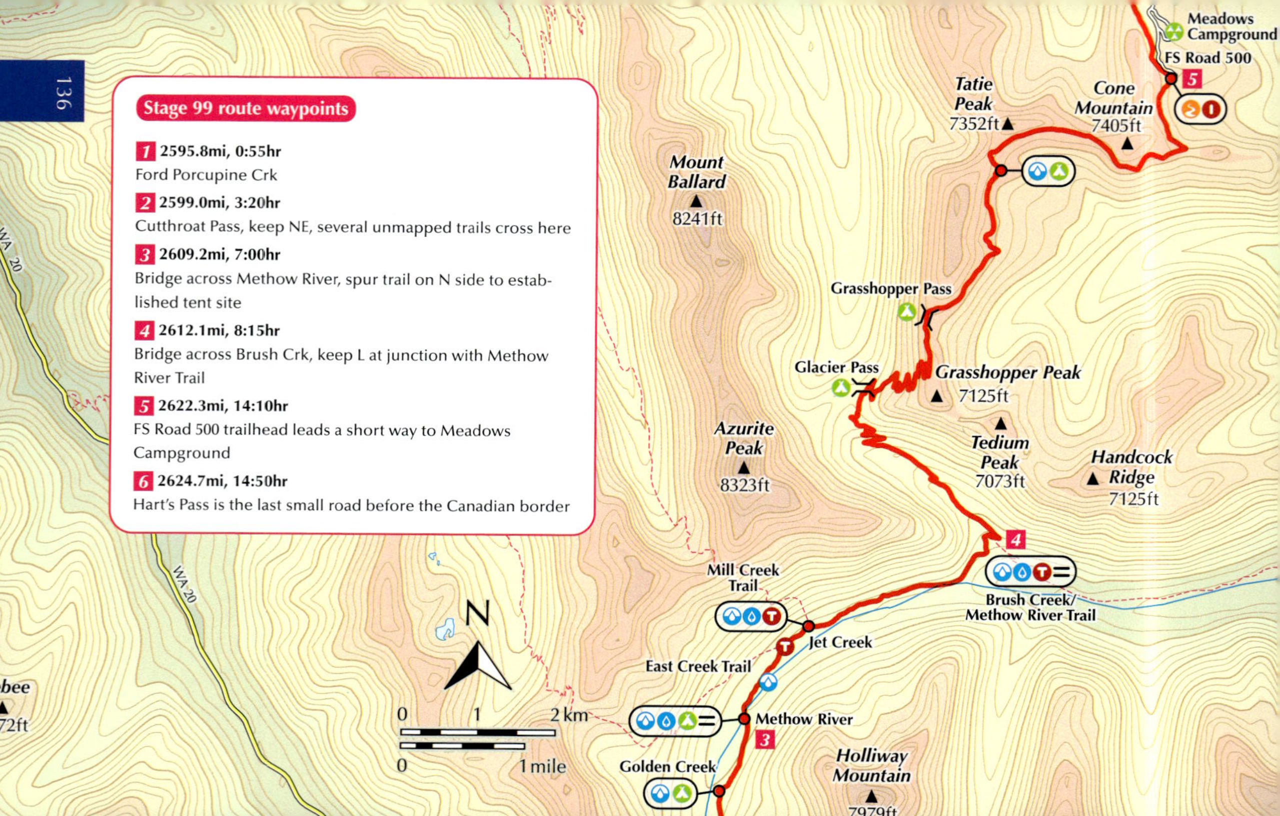

Stage 99 route waypoints

1 2595.8mi, 0:55hr
Ford Porcupine Crk

2 2599.0mi, 3:20hr
Cutthroat Pass, keep NE, several unmapped trails cross here

3 2609.2mi, 7:00hr
Bridge across Methow River, spur trail on N side to established tent site

4 2612.1mi, 8:15hr
Bridge across Brush Crk, keep L at junction with Methow River Trail

5 2622.3mi, 14:10hr
FS Road 500 trailhead leads a short way to Meadows Campground

6 2624.7mi, 14:50hr
Hart's Pass is the last small road before the Canadian border

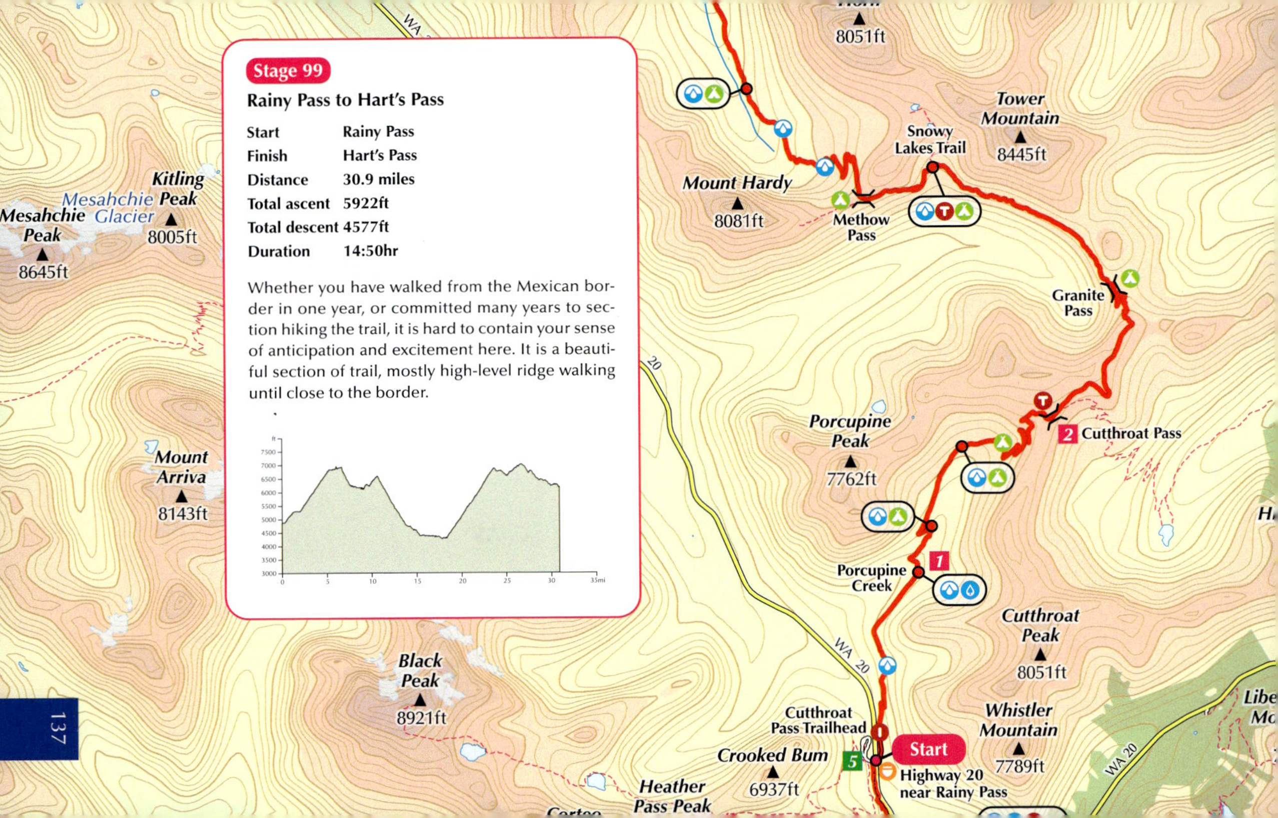

Stage 99

Rainy Pass to Hart's Pass

Start	Rainy Pass
Finish	Hart's Pass
Distance	30.9 miles
Total ascent	5922ft
Total descent	4577ft
Duration	14:50hr

Whether you have walked from the Mexican border in one year, or committed many years to section hiking the trail, it is hard to contain your sense of anticipation and excitement here. It is a beautiful section of trail, mostly high-level ridge walking until close to the border.

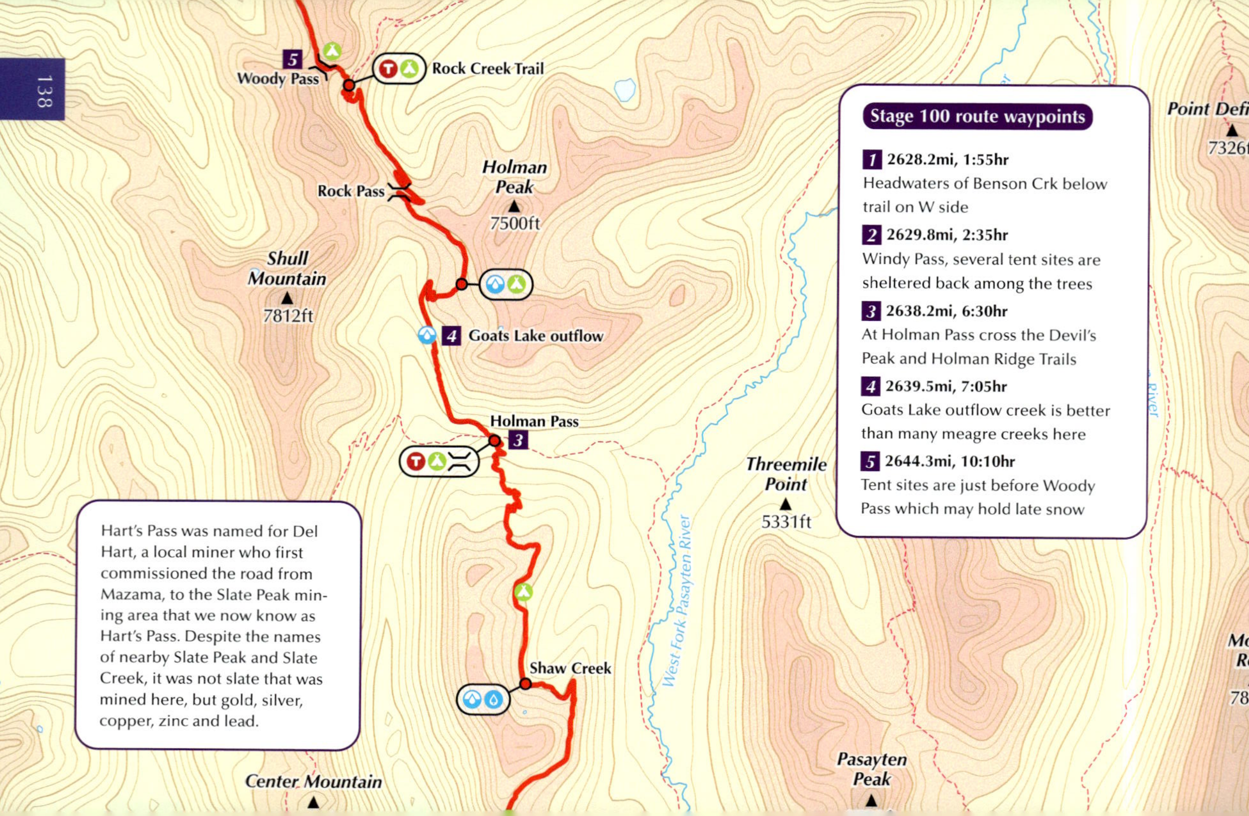

Stage 100 route waypoints

1 2628.2mi, 1:55hr
Headwaters of Benson Crk below trail on W side

2 2629.8mi, 2:35hr
Windy Pass, several tent sites are sheltered back among the trees

3 2638.2mi, 6:30hr
At Holman Pass cross the Devil's Peak and Holman Ridge Trails

4 2639.5mi, 7:05hr
Goats Lake outflow creek is better than many meagre creeks here

5 2644.3mi, 10:10hr
Tent sites are just before Woody Pass which may hold late snow

Hart's Pass was named for Del Hart, a local miner who first commissioned the road from Mazama, to the Slate Peak mining area that we now know as Hart's Pass. Despite the names of nearby Slate Peak and Slate Creek, it was not slate that was mined here, but gold, silver, copper, zinc and lead.

Stage 100

Hart's Pass to Northern Terminus

Start	Hart's Pass
Finish	Northern Terminus
Distance	30.5 miles
Total ascent	4485ft
Total descent	6424ft
Duration	14:30hr

An easy final stage to the border along ridges that offer inspiring views but leave you a little exposed in bad weather. Water sources are limited and could be a problem in a dry year.

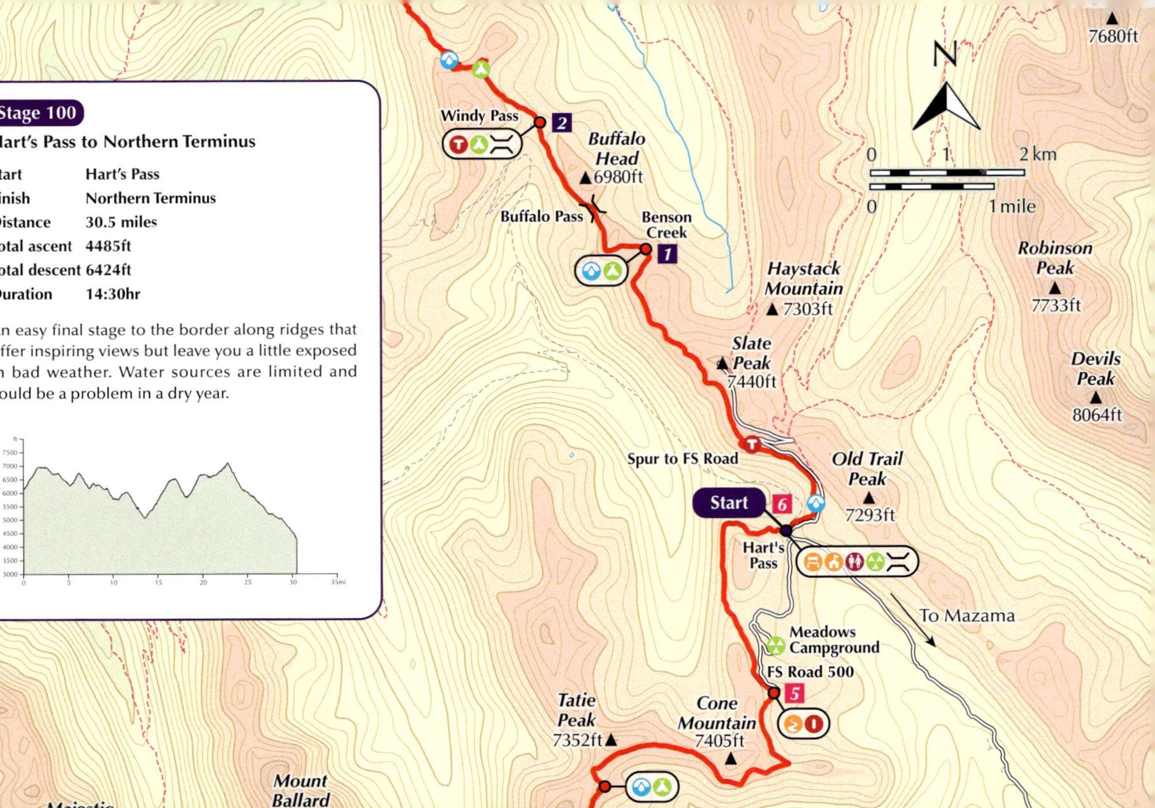

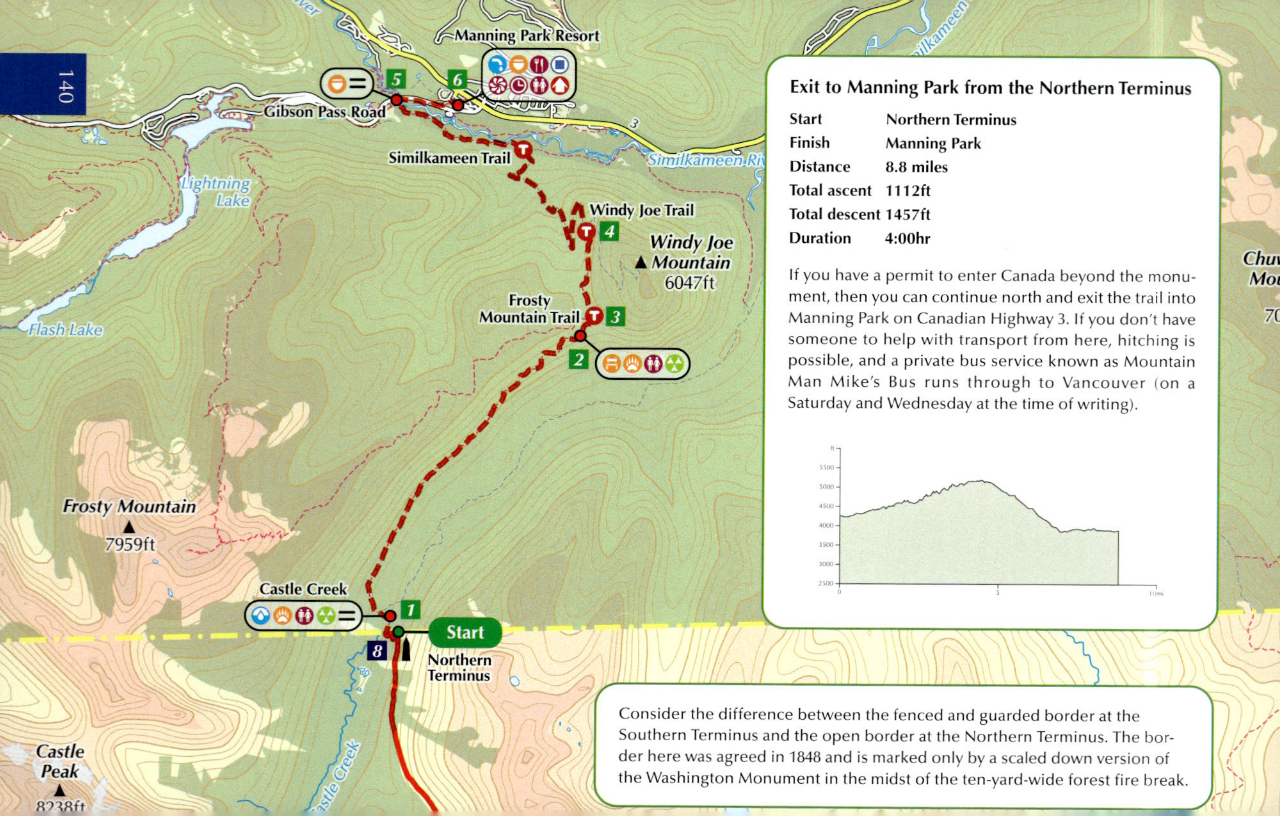

Exit to Manning Park from the Northern Terminus

Start	Northern Terminus
Finish	Manning Park
Distance	8.8 miles
Total ascent	1112ft
Total descent	1457ft
Duration	4:00hr

If you have a permit to enter Canada beyond the monument, then you can continue north and exit the trail into Manning Park on Canadian Highway 3. If you don't have someone to help with transport from here, hitching is possible, and a private bus service known as Mountain Man Mike's Bus runs through to Vancouver (on a Saturday and Wednesday at the time of writing).

Consider the difference between the fenced and guarded border at the Southern Terminus and the open border at the Northern Terminus. The border here was agreed in 1848 and is marked only by a scaled down version of the Washington Monument in the midst of the ten-yard-wide forest fire break.

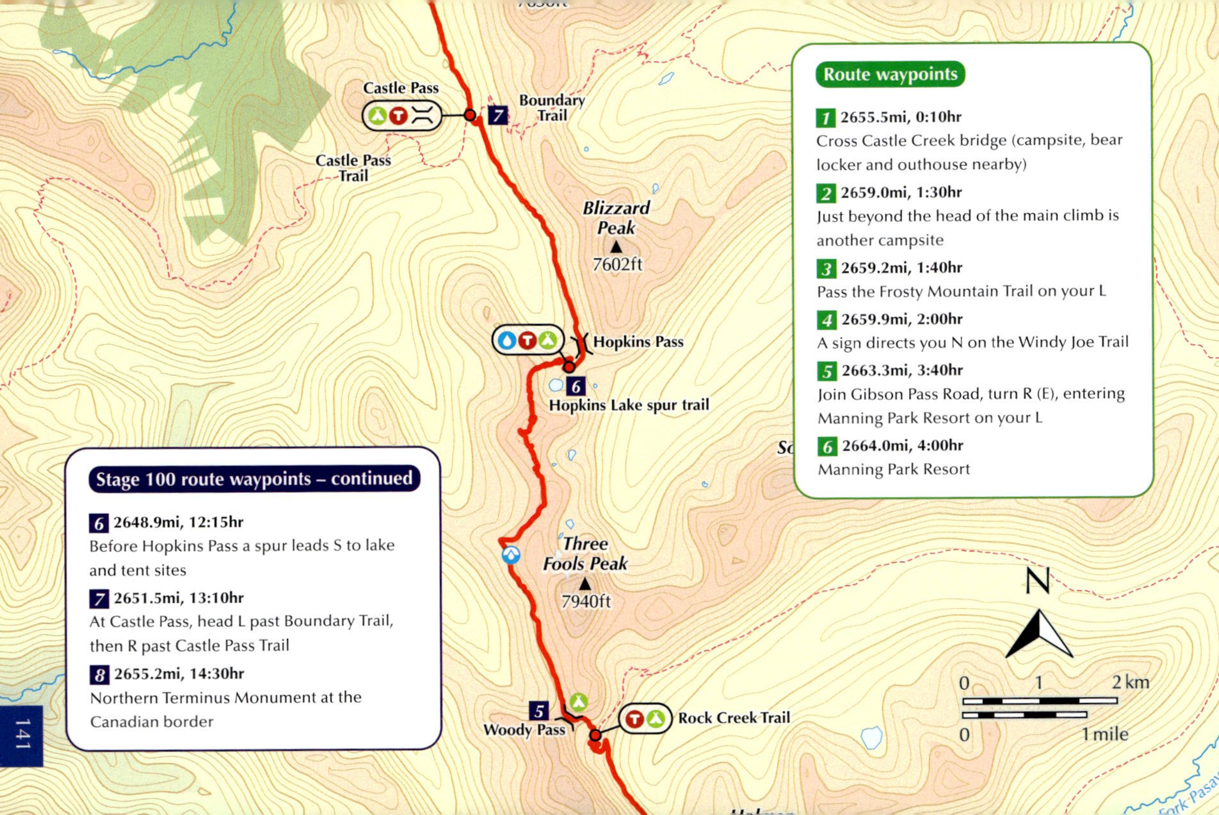

Stage 100 route waypoints – continued

6 2648.9mi, 12:15hr
Before Hopkins Pass a spur leads S to lake and tent sites

7 2651.5mi, 13:10hr
At Castle Pass, head L past Boundary Trail, then R past Castle Pass Trail

8 2655.2mi, 14:30hr
Northern Terminus Monument at the Canadian border

Route waypoints

1 2655.5mi, 0:10hr
Cross Castle Creek bridge (campsite, bear locker and outhouse nearby)

2 2659.0mi, 1:30hr
Just beyond the head of the main climb is another campsite

3 2659.2mi, 1:40hr
Pass the Frosty Mountain Trail on your L

4 2659.9mi, 2:00hr
A sign directs you N on the Windy Joe Trail

5 2663.3mi, 3:40hr
Join Gibson Pass Road, turn R (E), entering Manning Park Resort on your L

6 2664.0mi, 4:00hr
Manning Park Resort

NOTES

Clockwise from top left: Three Fingered Jack at dawn from the PCT (Stage 77); The historic Donomore Cabin close to the Oregon border (Stage 63); Water collects in 'terraces' after recent snow melt (Stage 60); Crater Lake (Stage 70); The glaciated Mount Adams (Stage 87)

The northern terminus monument at the Canadian border (Stage 100)